THE COUNTRY HOUSES
OF NORFOLK

PART ONE :
THE MAJOR HOUSES

David Clarke

The Country Houses of Norfolk

Part One:
The Major Houses

ISBN 0 900616 768

David Clarke
The Elms
19 Heigham Grove
Norwich NR2 3DQ

Printed and published by
Geo. R. Reeve Ltd.
9-11 Town Green, Wymondham, Norfolk, NR18 0BD

CONTENTS

INTRODUCTION

Popular interest in Country Houses remains at a high level. Great Houses, National Trust and privately owned alike, have their state rooms and servants, halls thrown open which attract the public in substantial numbers. Many houses, though smaller and not so grand but occupied by successive generations, open their gardens in aid of charity. The opportunity to meander around somebody else's beds and borders, with a peak through a downstairs window, proves irresistible to many at weekends from spring to autumn. The pages of Country Life and the windows of Savills and Strutt & Parker give a glimpse of a lifestyle of which many dream, but few can afford.

My schooldays in the fifties and sixties at Langley, a house then not long split from its estate but still with its park, gardens and stables (though with cricket squares, rugby goalposts and classrooms), left me with a deep-seated appreciation for the history and beauty of the buildings described in this volume. This interest has given rise to a local history collection, and in particular a country house archive, from which the following pages are drawn and which are intended to be an introduction to the larger Norfolk Country House as well as those, though perhaps less stately, that for many different reasons are of County importance. The contents, however, are arbitrary and 2 or 3 more volumes will be required to do justice to the subject (Burke's & Savills Guide to Country Houses, published in 1981, lists nearly 500 houses in the Norfolk section). All in good time; I am currently working on a volume of the 'lost houses of Norfolk' and compiling information about the country houses around Norwich.

The illustrations I have utilised are all from my collection, being mainly postcards of the 1900 to 1930 era, thus giving a snapshot of the days when the family at the big house was all important to the village and surrounding area. My sources are many and varied – the EDP, Country Life, sale catalogues, open leaflets, Norfolk Archaeology, the internet, biographies of family members and architectural works, both general and specific. For nearly every entry I have consulted the late George Winkley's 'The Country Houses of Norfolk' and volume III of Burke's & Savills (the Norfolk section being compiled by Michael Sayer). As with all research of a historical and genealogical nature, there is a tendency to follow that previously written and, inevitably, to compound any errors that exist in print. There are several instances where I have differed from the previous and where I have so done I have tried carefully to check and double check my facts.

The appendix lists the general sources of research and my primary sources for each entry. As this book is intended to be of general, rather than academic, interest I have not made use of extensive notes as to sources of minor reference.

BARNINGHAM HALL

The opening years of the seventeenth century saw the fortunes of the Pastons at their greatest. The struggles of the family as chronicled in the 'Paston Letters' were but a distant memory and for over a 100 years they had controlled large estates and lived in fine houses. The patriarch, Sir William Paston, had made his home at Paston, from whence the family name was derived, and at Caistor, the impressive brick castle, which had been built and bequeathed in the fifteenth century to an earlier Paston by Sir John Fastolf. Sir William, towards the end of his life, had also inherited Oxnead, the magnificent Tudor mansion, overlooking the River Bure, built by Clement Paston who had died in 1599. Other members of the family had built Appleton Hall near Sandringham (1596) and Barningham Hall (Sir Edward Paston, 1612).

By the 1730s the fortunes of the family had reversed. William Paston, the 2nd Earl of Yarmouth, died in 1732 leaving heavily mortgaged properties and enormous debts.

Lord Anson, the maritime explorer, purchased Paston (subsequently demolished) and Oxnead (much reduced), Caister had been sold by the mid 1600s and is a ruin and Appleton had been burnt in 1707. Barningham was abandoned by Edward Paston in 1736 and sold to settle his debts. It stands today, largely in its original form, the only remaining complete inhabited Paston house.

The Estate changed hands twice within a short space of time before being purchased in 1785 by Thomas Mott, ancestor to the present owners.

In 1807 Humphrey Repton, with his son John Adey Repton, was commissioned to remodel the south front and to make alterations to the interior. Watercolours, signed by the Reptons, showing the alterations remain in the family. It is probable that Humphrey Repton had also made improvements to the Park though no drawings exist. Before and after aquatints of the interior and exterior alterations are illustrated in their major work, 'Fragments on the theory of Landscape Gardening', published in 1816.

This imposing house, situated within its 4,000 acre Estate, can be seen from the road which runs between Saxthorpe and Sheringham.

BAYFIELD HALL

If you drive between Blakeney and Holt via Letheringsett you will pass on your left a fine long estate wall. If you are able to look over you will see the fine prospect, on rising ground, of an attractive rectangular red brick country house overlooking its lake with meadows and grazing. In a newspaper article the owner, Mr Robin Combe, told of his great fortune when he unexpectedly inherited the1,800 acre estate in 1960 from a great uncle. Originally he had let the hall, as he still does with cottages and the dower house, but moved in with his family in 1985.

The house that you now see beyond the wall took its present form in the latter part of the 18th century and incorporates part of an earlier 'E' plan house. This earlier house was acquired by the Jermys in the first half of the 17th century who owned it until 1766 when it was sold to trustees for Elizabeth the daughter and co-heir of Richard Warner of North Elmham and wife of Paul Jodrell. The Jodrells gave their name to the famous Jodrell Bank telescope, and another Elizabeth Jodrell was the grandmother of the famous 19th century novelist, Edward Bulwer-Lytton.

Bayfield became the home to Henry Jodrell, the youngest son of Elizabeth (nee Warner), who became an MP and Recorder for Great Yarmouth. The family (who also owned the estate at Salle) came into a baronetcy from a maternal uncle and, as far as Bayfield is concerned, the most prominent incumbent was the fourth and last baronet, Sir Alfred Jodrell (1847-1929). He was small of stature and had a very high pitched

Bayfield Hall.

voice but was very much a philanthropist. He was reported to have said, *"I intend to leave the estate in a better condition than when I inherited it"*, and it seems that he achieved his vow. He rebuilt the nearby village of Glandford and also the church, to the memory of his mother Adela Monckton Jodrell for whom he had also built the dower house (though she continued to live at the Hall). He had a fine collection of shells, and to house them, he built the Shell Museum in Glandford which remains open to the public to this day. He also benefited the churches at Letheringsett, Blakeney, Wiveton and Salle. Each week, he sent hampers of vegetables from the estate to the Norfolk and Norwich Hospital, and at Christmas, reportedly forty chickens and forty turkeys. He married late, his wife predeceased him, and as they had no children, the baronetcy became extinct. He left the estate to his godson, the Honourable Roger Coke, who was Robin Combe's Great Uncle.

BEESTON ST LAWRENCE HALL

Long home of the Prestons, Thomasine Preston, widow of Jacob Preston of Old Buckenham, purchased the Estate in 1640 from Edward Hobart the younger son of Sir Henry Hobart the builder of Blickling. The Hall that then stood, and which was engraved for Armstrong's History of Norfolk (published in 1781) was undoubtedly old fashioned and inconvenient and was replaced in 1786 by a Gothick style castellated knapped flint two storey house attributed to William Wilkins senior of Norwich. This was built for Jacob Preston who died from an heart attack at the age of 47 the following year. Though stylistically somewhat similar to its predecessor, the new house was better situated with views over the park and lake with the interiors varying in style from Gothick to Georgian.

Following the death of Jacob's widow in 1805, the Estate passed to his nephew, Thomas Hulton who took the name Preston by Royal Licence. He was the son of Elizabeth (Preston) and Henry Hulton who was commissioner for customs and excise at Boston in America at the time of 'The Boston Tea Party'. He returned to this country with his 4 American born younger brothers after the British defeat in the American War of Independence. He was a colonel in the East Norfolk Yeomanry, twice married and had 2 sons and 8 daughters, and was created a baronet in 1815.

His heir, the 2nd baronet, was another Jacob who spent his life on Estate and County affairs, he was a keen yachtsman and sailed the famous lateen rigged 'Maria' which was accepted as the fastest yacht on the Broads. The Maria can be seen displayed at the Museum of the Broads.

The 6th baronet, Sir Thomas, succeeded his cousin Lt Col Sir Edward Hulton Preston in 1963 when he was 77 years of age. He had had an adventurous early life overseas – as a young man he had prospected for gold in Siberia and later, whilst in the diplomatic service, he was a consul in Russia at the time of the murder of the Tsar and Imperial family by the Bolsheviks. His attempts to protect them earned him a death sentence, from which he was saved by a timely interception by friendly forces.

The current and 7th baronet, Sir Ronald, opened the house to the public until relatively recently before, in 1994, placing the house and estate of 575 acres on the market for 1.5 million pounds.

BLICKLING HALL

Blickling Hall.

The shear awe-inspiring beauty of an English country house – mellow red brick, turrets, clock tower, leaded windows, outstretched low wings with venerable yew hedges embracing gravel paths and manicured lawns, all fronted with wrought iron gates and railings. This is Blickling, one of the finest Jacobean halls in the land.

The estate and manor has passed through several hands significant to the history of Norfolk – Sir Thomas Erpingham, Sir John Fastolfe, Geoffrey Boleyn, Sir Edward Clere – to name but four, before Sir Henry Hobart, the first baronet, purchased in 1616 and had the present house (re)built to designs by Robert Lyminge, the builder of Hatfield House. There is of course no truth in the widely held belief that Anne Boleyn, second wife of Henry VIII and mother to Queen Elizabeth, was born in this house, though her father did hold the estate at the time of her birth and it is possible that this could have taken place in a previous hall.

Sir Henry did not live to see his house completed, that was left to his son, Sir John, and the house that he inherited and completed cost the family over £10,000 (perhaps, though, only a quarter of the cost of the stylistically similar but larger Hatfield for the Cecils).

The third and fourth baronets, Sir John (d 1683) and Sir Henry, were both politically inclined, and the latter came to an untimely end in 1698 as a result of rumours emanating from the recent general election.

THE TOWER, BLICKLING PARK.

Incensed that his defeat at the poll was because of allegations put about of his conduct at the Battle of the Boyne, where he acted as an equerry to William III, he challenged his Tory opponent, Oliver Le Neve, to a duel on Cawston Heath. He was 'run through' and died at Blickling the next day, his heir being his 5 year old son, John. This John was enobled as Baron Hobart in 1728 and created the first Earl of Buckinghamshire in 1745. His son, the second earl and another John (1723-93), employed the Norwich architect, and builder of the Octagon Chapel and Assembly House in the City, Thomas Ivory, with his son William, to make considerable internal and external alterations and additions including the west and north fronts. The renowned country house architect, Samuel Wyatt, was also employed in the early 1780s to design the Orangery, which can be seen from the Aylsham road.

On the second Earl's death in 1793, the title passed to his brother George. The estate, however, was inherited by his second daughter Caroline who had married William Harbord, the heir to the barony of Suffield and to the nearby Gunton estate. Caroline's elder sister, Harriet, was out of favour having twice married, the second time to the Earl of Ancram, later the 6th Marquis of Lothian. Caroline and William remained childless so, on Lord Suffield's death in 1821, the Lothians inherited but were unable to take up possession until Lady Suffield died, at the age of 83, in 1850.

The 8th Marquis, William Schomberg Robert Kerr, was only nine years of age when he inherited the title in 1841, and eighteen when he came to Blickling, but by 1856 plans were underway to remodel rooms and to provide up to date facilities. William Burn was employed to rebuild the west wing, retaining only the existing front wall, in order to provide new offices and accommodation for servants. The Marquis died at the young age of 38 and, on the death in 1901 of his widow, Blickling ceased to be a home and was let to tenants for the next thirty years, inevitably becoming somewhat rundown. Records show that at the time of the death of the 10th Marquis in 1930, the house was let to a Mr G. Russell, a cousin of the Duke of Bedford, who paid £1,200 furnished plus £300 for certain shooting. The preceding tenant, who took up occupation in 1927, was a Mrs Hoffman, an American lady, who agreed to £1,575 plus £246 for insurance.

In 1932, the 11th Marquis and Liberal politician, Philip Kerr, decided to make Blickling his principal English seat. He had inherited several estates in both England and Scotland including those of Montevoit, Newbattle Abbey, Ferniehirst Castle and of course Blickling. Montevoit was to be the family home, Newbattle a college and Ferniehirst a youth hostel. There remained Blickling where little had been spent since the 19th century. Cottages were in poor condition with bad feeling locally, and the Hall itself cluttered, drab and needing a family presence. The Marquis decided to exploit Blickling's beauty as a refuge where he and

The Mausoleum, Blickling Park

his friends could escape from London for short periods. Thus it was used, with a full compliment of staff, and with groups of well known figures from the political scene weekending with meetings, discussions and shooting. Much money needed to be spent on the house and the estate, and this was put in hand, but the burden of death duties was pressing which lead to the reluctant sale of some of the most valuable books from the library at auction in New York in 1932. This realised £102,225, every penny of which went to the Exchequer.

It was Lord Lothian's concern that future death duties could result in the splitting of the house from the estate and lead to decline with lack of access for the public. It was his determination, *"that it should be used not only as a private residence but as a place from which public or intellectual or artistic activities go forth,"* that led to his address to the National Trust's annual meeting in 1934 where he set out the basis of what was to become the 'Country House Scheme' whereby many fine houses with their estates were passed to the Trust, intact and self-supporting. A parliamentary bill was passed to this effect in 1937. On Lord Lothian's death in 1940, in New York where he was Ambassador, Blickling passed to the National Trust, being the first of what has become the many.

Currently the estate comprises just under 4,800 acres including 500 of woodland, 450 of parkland, 3,500 farmland, and of course the gardens and lake. Farms and cottages are situated in the surrounding parishes, particularly Blickling, Oulton, Itteringham, Ingworth and Aylsham. The Buckinghamshire Arms public house, Aylsham Old Hall (acquired in 1751), Blickling Lodge close to Ingworth (purchased in 1839) and Aylsham marketplace itself are all part of the estate. The Old Hall and the Lodge have both been sold on long leases. Other notable buildings include the Gothic Tower which was built in the 1770s by Lord Buckinghamshire for use as a grandstand to watch racing (it was converted for residential use in 1857), and the Mausoleum, England's first pyramid, built in 1796 by Joseph Bonomi to house the body of the 2nd earl and, subsequently, his two countesses.

CROMER HALL

Cromer Hall.   Ranner & Wortley's Series,

The knapped flint house that stands today was built in the Gothick style in 1829 for George Thomas Wyndham by the architect William Donthorne. It replaced a similar house built only two years previously but destroyed by fire. This in turn replaced an irregular gabled house built at least 100 years earlier, possibly for Sir George Wyndham. Latterly, at least, the Wyndhams (who were distantly related to the Windhams of Felbrigg) did not live there but presumably, as was common in those days, let. From about 1820 the earlier house was rented by the Fowell Buxtons and provided an autumn retreat for Thomas Fowell Buxton, member of parliament and slave trade abolitionist, from his political exertions. He and his wife shared the house with his sister-in-law, Priscilla Gurney who died there of TB in 1821, and also the Hoares who were also in the habit of passing the autumn months at Cromer.

The new house was also probably let as Evelyn Baring, of the Baring Brothers Banking family, was born there in 1841, the son of Henry Baring and his wife Cecilia, daughter of Admiral William Windham of Felbrigg Hall. Evelyn was, in 1901, created the 1st Earl of Cromer.

The Wyndhams sold the estate in 1852 to Benjamin Bond-Cabbell who died in 1874. His widow, Margaret, and son, Benjamin Bond, were responsible in 1891 for auctioning 72 building plots and a site for an hotel on part of the estate to the west of the town and south of the coast road.

Arthur Conan Doyle, whilst recuperating from fever contracted in South Africa, stayed in the area in March 1901. Here he learnt about the legend of 'Black Shuck', the giant dog with huge eyes that glowed like coals, and whose tracks led into the grounds of the hall. It is said that he based Baskerville Hall in 'The Hound of the Baskervilles' on the hall that he had seen at Cromer.

In order to maintain the hall, the present owner, Benjamin Cabbell Manners, has in recent times attempted diversification for parts of the estate with plans to convert farm buildings to industrial use, create a garden centre, and recently, allow a part to be used as a zoo.

DITCHINGHAM HALL

This attractive well proportioned Queen Anne House, situated within its Capability Brown Park, provides a glimpse of the quintessential English country house when seen from the Norwich to Bungay road.

It is of two periods, with the early 18th century 7 bay south front overlooking the lake with 5 bays to the west which were added to in an

identical style by William Carr in the early part of the 20th century with the addition of 4 bays and the central stone porch.

When built, the house was the seat of the Bedingfields and it was purchased by the Carrs in the 1880s. It is now the home of the 13th Earl and Countess Ferrers, Lady Ferrers being the daughter of Brigadier Carr (died 1981), the son of the William Carr who was responsible for the enlargement of the house. Earl Ferrers is a former Conservative minister and Deputy Leader of the House of Lords, in which he retains his seat.

The Baron de Ferrers came over in 1066 with William the Conqueror and was given land near Chartley in Staffordshire. It was during the reign of Henry III, and following enclosure of part of the forest of Needwood, that saw the beginnings of the Chartley herd of cattle which remained there until 1905. The herd now thrives at Ditchingham under the supervision of the 13th Earl.

Within the house hangs a portrait of George Washington, the first president of the United States, whose ancestor was Elizabeth Washington, the 1st Countess Ferrers.

EAST BARSHAM MANOR

Described by Pevsner as, *"a picturesque ideal of an early Tudor house, which is too good to be true when one first sets eyes on it"*, this outstanding example of English Tudor brick domestic architecture with its

freestanding two storey crenellated gatehouse dates from the first half of the 15th century.

It was built for Sir Henry Fermor, descended to the Calthorpes in about 1628 and 100 years later to the L'Estranges, and then in the 1760s, through their co-heirs, to the Astleys of Melton Constable. By this time much decay had set in and its use was probably as a farmhouse. By Victorian times, the west wing had become ruinous with little more than the façade and fine stack of ten chimneys still

standing (happily now all restored). Lord Hastings sold the house in 1914 to a Mr Coleman who commenced restorations by 1919. The Colemans put the house and estate of just over 1,000 acres up for sale in 1935, and it has subsequently been in several different ownerships. At one time, in the 1960s, rumour had it that a member of the Rolling Stones had purchased for a weekend retreat-in fact it was a director of the management company behind The Bee Gees and Cream who had acquired it in 1967 for about £20,000. Presumably by that time the estate had largely gone, as when the present owners, Sir John and Lady Guinness, bought the house it stood in only 7 acres.

It is said that Henry VIII and his Queen, Catherine of Aragon, stayed there when the King made, barefoot, a pilgrimage to the

Shrine at Walsingham to pray for the life of his sickly son. Queen Mary, wife of George V, was a visitor in 1938, presumably whilst she was staying at Sandringham.

FELBRIGG HALL

The Book: 'Felbrigg: The Story of a House' has continually been in print since Robert Wyndham Ketton-Cremer, the compiler and last squire, saw it published in 1962. It was he who bequeathed the estate to the National Trust following his death in 1969, being the last in a line of owners of local or national interest. The book tells the story of:-

William Windham (died 1689), who together with his wife Katherine, conscientiously ran the Estate and most importantly kept records which today gives us an insight into the happenings of over 300 years ago. It was he who commissioned William Samwell to design the fine West Wing.

William Windham II (d 1761), away on the Grand Tour from 1738-42 and inheriting from his father, Ashe Windham, in 1749 married Sarah Lukin in 1750 when she was 40 and pregnant with their heir, having had 3 children from her previous marriage. He was intent on domestic harmony and improvement to the House.

Their only son, William Windham III (d 1810), active in politics, associate of Humphrey Repton, 7 years Secretary at War, Chief Secretary to the Lord Lieutenant of Ireland and friend of Samuel Johnson, some of whose books remain in the Felbrigg Library. It is said that William still returns from time to time to consult the volumes of his old friend.

Vice Admiral Lukin (d 1833), who prior to inheriting from his Uncle, made a name for himself as Captain of the Mars in actions against the French. He later assumed the name of Windham.

His son, William Howe Windham (d 1854) who invested in the farms on the Estate and built the Cromer Lodges. He married Lady Sophia Hervey (of Ickworth) and, not unsurprisingly considering the eccentricities of the Hervey Line, his son, William Frederick, became known as 'Mad Windham' despite being found sane by the Courts following his Uncle's petition for De Lunatico Inquirendo in 1861.

From his boyhood, William Frederick had a love for uniforms which at various times saw him take on the unofficial roles of train station guard, policeman in London and before his death in 1866, the somewhat alarming driver of an express coach plying between Norwich and Cromer. His Bankers were forced to foreclose on the Estate in 1863 which was then sold to John Ketton a Norwich merchant.

The Kettons, who were unexceptional owners and who by 1924 had passed the Estate to a nephew, Wyndham Cremer, of Beeston Hall near Sheringham, who later took the name Wyndham Ketton-Cremer. By accident or design this was a branch of the Wyndhams of Cromer (see Cromer Hall) who were descended from the builder of Felbrigg back in the 17th century. Their eldest son was Robert Wyndham Ketton-Cremer, the last Squire.

Apart from the Estate, his legacy was in his writings – major biographies on Horace Walpole and Thomas Grey, as well as a number of published works of essays about local figures and events from, in the main, 18th century Norfolk.

Of more recent interest are the three books by Mary Mackie, the wife of the House Administrator at the time, which tell of life in a National Trust House in the 1990s.

GILLINGHAM HALL

Sir Nicholas Bacon, the 1st baronet of Gillingham, built the 17th century house that stands close to the Norfolk Suffolk border near to Beccles. The Norfolk Bacons can be very confusing – Stiffkey, Raveningham, Gillingham, Earlham – Nicholas, Nathaniel, Edmund, Francis – Knights, Baronets, Barons and so on.

It goes something like this: Sir Nicholas Bacon (Knight-died 1579) was the Lord Keeper of the Great Seal in the reign of Queen Elizabeth and married twice. His eldest son was also named Nicholas (d 1624) and in 1611 he was the first ever created baronet (of Redgrave in Suffolk) and it is this line that remains today at Raveningham as the Premier baronets. His second son was Nathaniel (d 1622) who built the hall at Stiffkey and whose first wife was a Gresham. Sir Nicholas's youngest son by his second wife was the famous Francis Bacon (d 1626), philosopher, essayist and Lord Chancellor. He was created 1st Baron Verulam and later Viscount St Alban.

Sir Nicholas, the premier baronet, had five sons:-

(1) Sir Edmund the 2nd baronet, (2) Sir Robert the 3rd baronet, (3) Sir Butts who was named after his mother's family, and was created the 1st Mildenhall baronet (and which is now incorporated into the Raveningham line), (4) Nicholas for whom the estate at Gillingham was purchased, and who had a son, also named Nicholas (d 1666), who was created the 1st baronet of Gillingham in 1661, and (5) Sir Nathaniel knight of Culford in

Suffolk who became an eminent painter.

When Sir Nicholas, the builder of Gillingham, died in 1666 he was succeeded by his sons, firstly Edmund the 2nd baronet, and then Richard the 3rd and last baronet who had married his cousin Anne, the daughter of Sir Henry Bacon the 2nd baronet of Mildenhall. After his death in 1685, the estate passed to his wife's family and through the female line successively to Susan Schutz (nee Bacon), the Beresfords, Kenyons (who built the chapel), Todhunters and Bramleys.

In 1999 Robin Bramley put the house, with 1,227 acres, up for sale at an asking price in excess of 6 million pounds, and in 2000, the house with just 45 acres was offered for 1.25 million pounds. In 2005, and now owned by a middle eastern gentleman, the house, chapel, stables and lake with 55 acres were again placed on the market for 2.25 million pounds, and I understand have since sold.

GREAT WITCHINGHAM HALL

Some houses are notable for their outstanding architecture, others for the famous families who lived within, but in the case of Great Witchingham it is for turkeys! Seen as the backdrop to TV adverts for Bernard Matthews Plc with the well known catchphrase 'Bootiful', it has played its part in the romantic 'self-made man' story of Bernard Matthews who at the age of 21 acquired an incubator and 10 rented acres with an idea of hatching turkey eggs. The rest is history.

Great Witchingham Hall, a 30 bedroom rundown pile in about 30 acres, was bought for £30,000 by Bernard Matthews in 1957 ostensibly as a turkey house. It is said that the eggs were incubated in the Elizabethan dining room, reared in the Jacobean bedrooms and processed in the Victorian kitchens. Such unconventional uses generally led to the demise and eventual demolition of country houses, but in the case of Great Witchingham the opposite is the case. Given the fashion at that time, without the turkeys, the hall may well not still be standing today.

It is no longer a turkey shed but restored palatial offices and a home. The hall as it is today consists of much 19th century remodelling/building around the central 16/17th century core. Then it was owned by celebrated antiquaries, the Le Neves*, later sold to John Norris and passed through the Wodehouses of Kimberley until sold around 1800 to the Thompsons

who carried out much of the rebuilding. Following several changes of ownership, the estate was eventually split up in 1952.

* In 1698 at Cawston, Oliver Le Neve, against his will and fighting left-handed, fought a famous duel with Sir Henry Hobart of Blickling, the result leading to the latter's death and Le Neve's exile abroad.

GUNTON HALL

The core of the present house was built in the mid 1740s for Sir William Harbord, the 1st baronet, by Norwich architect/builder Matthew Brettingham. It was trebled in size from 1775 by the Wyatt brothers for Sir William's son, Sir Harbord Harbord who was created the 1st Baron Suffield. The south Brettingham front overlooked an 1800 acre park with its two lakes, all within a 12,000 acre estate – it was said that one could travel from Cromer to the outskirts of Norwich and yet not put foot on another person's land. Building and estate improvements continued under the 2nd & 3rd barons whilst the 5th, Charles Harbord, was much in favour at Court becoming Lord of the Bedchamber to the Prince of Wales (later Edward VII) and Lord in Waiting to both Queen Victoria and Edward. He was chief of the Prince of Wales' Household in Edward's momentous tour of India in 1875/6 and the Prince visited the estate many times and in fact lived there in 1869 whilst Sandringham was being rebuilt.

The 5th baron's expenses often exceeded his income and for many years he let the house for the shooting. It was whilst let in 1882 that a chimney fire caused the Brettingham wing, with its major reception rooms, library and bedrooms above, to become a blackened ruin. Blocked off from the remainder, it in fact so remained for over 100 years, only being restored relatively recently.

Gunton never really regained its former splendour and with the death of the 8th baron, John Harbord in 1945, the title passed to a kinsman with

the Honourable Doris Harbord, the elder daughter of the 6th baron, remaining at Gunton. Her death in 1980 closed one chapter but opened the way for a new beginning – Irelands held a famous 5 day Country House Sale at the house in the September, with the proceeds exceeding one million pounds. They also sold lodges and cottages by auction, with a further 20 lot auction of land and cottages held in 1982. The house, then almost ruinous, was sold by the Trustees to Kit Martin who specialised in sympathetically splitting large neglected country houses into more manageable dwellings. This has long been successfully completed including the restoration of the fire-damaged south wing.

Close by, to the east, is the now redundant former parish church designed in 1769 by Robert Adam. In the Grecian style, it remains as Adam's only Norfolk commission.

THE TOWER, GUNTON PARK.

The Tower Gunton Park

Completed in 1830 for Edward 3rd Baron Suffield as an observatory with accommodation beneath, the tower came into its own later in that year when riots against agricultural mechanisation were prevalent in Norfolk. A mob was threatening the water-powered saw mill (now restored by the Norfolk Windmills Trust and operated by the Norfolk Industrial Archaeological Society). Lord Suffield had a reputation as a good employer and had support of over 100 of his men, armed with stout cudgels, to defend his property. The flying of a red flag at the top of the tower was to be the signal to assemble at their stations. Later, in court, when asked why the rioters did not attack – one replied, *"why, my Lord, we saw your bloody flag which we knew was to be the sign that you would give no quarter; we knew your courage, and we dare not encounter you"*.

Following virtual dereliction, the tower has been restored, with great care and considerable expense, into living accommodation.

HANWORTH HALL

A well proportioned handsome house built for 'Squire' Robert Doughty in about 1700, possibly to replace an earlier hall destroyed by fire.

The Doughtys* who had resided here for several centuries appear to have been in business as merchants trading overseas. A near neighbour, Humphrey Repton the landscape gardener, gave advise on the park and also provided the likeness of the house for the engraving that appeared in Armstrong's History of Norfolk, published in 1781. Around 1740 Matthew Brettingham, the Norwich architect, was employed to make internal alterations – the exterior remaining much the same today as to when it was built over 300 years ago.

With the death of Robert Lee Doughty in 1819, the line came to an end.

The estate passed via inheritance to Vice-Admiral W.F. Lukin who also inherited Felbrigg and took the name Windham. Following the demise of Mad Windham (see Felbrigg Hall), the Hanworth estate was eventually sold by 1900 to the Barclays, a branch of the family probably best known for the bank of the same name. It remains a Barclay seat.

*   In 1687 William Doughty founded Doughty's Hospital in Norwich for twenty-four poor men and eight poor women.*

HEYDON HALL

HEYDON HALL, FRONT VIEW

In a county of great estates, Holkham, Houghton and Sandringham to name but three, Heydon stands out as a jewel with its family, venerable hall, park, gardens and estate, the church, and the village with the grange and dower house, the cottages, pub and blacksmiths, all designated as a conservation area as long ago as 1971 at a time when demolition and downsizing were still the order of the day.

How different it could have been, for in 1970 the then heir, William Bulwer-Long, a serving Captain in the Lancers, was given advice to knock down the Hall, sell the land along with the freeholds of all the village houses, invest the capital and enjoy the rest of his life. The County is eternally grateful that the Captain was made of sterner stuff, and though he died at the age of 59 in 1996, he had completed much that he had set out to do – the Hall made habitable including demolishing the Victorian additions (seen in the photo to the right and the left), farming the estate, planting thousands of trees and modernising the cottages.

The house dates from 1582 and was built for Henry Dynne, an auditor of the Exchequer, who died soon after. It was then sold twice before being purchased in about 1640 by Erasmus Earle, a Cromwellian lawyer from Salle (Oliver Cromwell visited on more than one occasion). It came to the Bulwers in 1576 on the marriage of Mary Earle, an heiress to Heydon, and William Wiggett Bulwer. The Bulwers had built and lived at Wood Dalling Hall nearby though this has since been sold off. The Heydon estate has subsequently passed from Bulwer to Bulwer, confusingly most being named William, until today.

The famous prolific 19th century author, Lord Lytton (of Knebworth) was the youngest son of General and Elizabeth (nee Warburton and heir to Knebworth) Bulwer and was brought up at Heydon. The eldest son, William, succeeded to the Bulwer estates, the middle son, Henry, became a politician and diplomat and was created Lord Dalling, and Edward the youngest, on the General's death in 1807, moved with his mother to Knebworth. He took the name Bulwer-Lytton, inherited Knebworth after his mother died in 1843, and was enobled in 1866 as Baron Lytton of Knebworth. Jane Preston, in 1998, wrote a book about the life of Elizabeth called, 'That Odd Rich old Woman'. This is now out of print but still in print is her second book, 'The Squires of Heydon Hall', published in 2003. This tells the story of the family and estate from the earliest times through to the present.

The village remains today as not only a living community, but also the setting for films and TV dramas undoubtedly bringing in much needed revenue to the estate. Benjamin Earle Bulwer-Long, the son of the late Captain Bulwer-Long, now resides at Heydon Hall with his wife Rhona.

HILBOROUGH HALL

A not unattractive 5 bay x 3 bay Georgian House built in 1779 for Lord of the Manor Ralph Caldwell* who was a steward at Holkham for Thomas Coke, 1st Earl of Leicester. An engraving of the newly built house can be seen in volume six of Armstrong's History of Norfolk published in 1781. At this time Admiral (and later Baron Nelson of the Nile and Hilborough) Nelson's father was rector here before moving to Burnham Thorpe. In fact from 1734 to 1806 every rector was a Nelson with one exception, and he had married into the family.

For a short period in the middle of the 19th century the estate was owned by the Duke of Wellington, and by the early 1860s, it had been acquired by the Mills family. It remained the family seat until the death of Mrs Betty Mills in 1985. In the introduction to the Christies auction catalogue for the sale of the contents (which realised £850,000), a family friend describes the comfort and style in which Major and Mrs Charles Mills lived at Hilborough. Staff waited at table and every comfort was provided for their guests who included members of the Royal Family for the pheasant shooting

The estate with the mansion, 6 farms, 17 cottages, 500 acres of woodland including the shoots, in all 6,436 acres, was put up for sale by private treaty in 1985 at a guide price of six million pounds. Early interest by the army for an extension to the battle area was not followed up and, by December, 3 buyers had been found including G.D. Bowes & Sons of Watton. They purchased 2,000 acres which included the house which was put back on the market with 40 acres at an asking price of £600,000. In May 1986 the trustees held a further 16 lot auction of properties within the village.

It seems that despite, since 1741, having been a trusted steward to Lord Leicester, and after his death, a trustee of the will, Cauldwell may well have financed Hilborough by 'filling his own pockets at the expense of his employer' ('Holkham' published by Prestel, page 47).

HOLKHAM HALL

In 2005, Prestel published a book edited by Leo Schmidt, Christian Keller and Polly Feversham entitled 'Holkham'. For anybody with an interest in the hall, the estate, the grand tour, the family or generally the country house today, it is certainly £30 well spent.

It tells the story of Thomas Coke (1697-1759) who on undertaking the grand tour, purchased antiques, fine art and sculpture, for showing in a new grand mansion that he was to build at Holkham to replace the old fashioned existing Hill Hall on the prosperous family estate that he inherited at the age of ten and took possession of in 1718. He was created

Earl of Leicester in 1744 but was to die before seeing the house completed, this responsibility being taken by his Countess, Margaret. Matthew Brettingham, the Norwich architect/builder, was responsible for overseeing the construction, but perhaps took rather too much credit for the design and was discharged by Margaret when she took control.

With their son predeceasing them, the estate passed to a nephew, Wenman Roberts, who had taken the name Coke, and on his death in 1776, to his son Thomas William Coke, later the 1st Earl of Leicester of the 2nd creation. He was 'Coke of Norfolk' the great agriculturist and instigator of the famous annual sheep shearings. After he died in 1842, a public subscription was raised and £5,409 spent on erecting the Monument to his memory which can be seen beyond the cricket field to the north front.

The Fountain, Holkham Hall

Today, Holkham remains a great estate of some 25,000 acres. With its mansion, innumerable lodges, cottages, farmhouses and estate buildings to keep up, farming no longer suffices to pay all the bills. Diversification has been essential, and under the heir to the estate, Thomas Viscount Coke (b 1965), this is being achieved with such diverse enterprises as the pottery, the ancient house, the bygones, the beach and holiday parks, the Victoria Hotel (and now the Globe in Wells), all in addition to the traditional estate activities.

HONING HALL

Honing is a fine example of the smaller country house being built in the 18th century for the gentry of Norfolk. It was completed in 1748 for Andrew Chamber, a Norwich Worsted Weaver, at a cost of probably no more than £1,000 (Holkham cost £92,000).

Financial difficulties led to its sale within a few years to the Cubitts who were well established in the area. Clearly the new owners, in the fashion of the day, wished to improve their house and park, and in 1788 Country House architect, John Soane, was employed to draw up plans for internal and external alterations of which the two storey bowed bay to the west front, is the most visually evident. Three of the original drawings survive at the house, and for these Soane charged 12 guineas.

In the spring of 1792, the landscape gardener, Humphrey Repton was commissioned to draw up plans for improvements to the park and grounds and he produced a most attractive Red Book illustrating and describing the 'before and after'. Much was carried out including alterations to the cornice and provision of a string course to the house itself. Repton also provided a view of the house for an engraving which embellished the 1794 edition of Peacock's Polite Repository, a popular lady's diary of the time.

The house remains as the family seat.

HOUGHTON HALL

   Norfolk is blessed to have two great stately homes, palaces almost, both built in the first half of the 18th century by members of long-standing county families and still so owned. Whereas Holkham is brick and plain, some might even say austere, Houghton, faced with stone and with its corner domes and flanking wings, is almost perfect and certainly fit for entertaining and showing by the great statesman that was Robert Walpole. He was Britain's de facto first Prime Minister, in office between 1721 and 1742, and with power and patronage at his disposal was able to afford the in excess of £200,000 (an estimate as he had reputably destroyed the bills) that Houghton had cost.

   The house was designed by Colin Campbell with the building work entrusted to Thomas Ripley, a carpenter by trade, who went on to design Wolterton for Robert's brother Horatio and also the Admiralty at Whitehall. Sir Robert, created Earl of Orford in 1742, died in 1745, and was succeeded by his son and then by his grandson, George the 3rd earl, in 1751. By this time the estate had become greatly indebted and George was prone to bouts of insanity. It was he who sold his grandfather's great art collection to the Empress Catherine of Russia for £40,000 which today can still be seen at the Hermitage Museum in St Petersburgh. He died childless and Horace Walpole of Strawberry Hill at Twickenham, Sir Robert's youngest brother, inherited the title and estate. He was a bachelor, letter writer and confident, and in his mid 70s, was a reluctant inheritor but took his responsibilities seriously. With his heir, George the 4th earl and later 1st marques of Cholmondeley (and grandson of Mary, Sir Robert's only daughter), the estate was saved.

It was not until after the 1st world war that Houghton again took on the roll as a home. In the 19th century it had been offered to the Duke of Wellington after Waterloo, but it was turned down for Stratfield Saye. It was considered for the Prince of Wales but nearby Sandringham was chosen instead. It was put up for auction with 10,000 acres in 1886 but was not sold. In 1919 the 5th marques, who had married Sybil Sassoon whose brother Philip was a millionaire, politician and aesthete and cousin the famous war poet Siegfried, took up residence and, until Sybil's death in 1989, devoted themselves to Houghton's well being. This work continues, and today under David, the 7th marques, this magnificent house is again in first class condition.

HUNSTANTON HALL

The Hall E., Old Hunstanton

Hunstanton, both old and new, is synonymous with the Le Strange family who have been estate owners since the 12th century. The moated crenellated flint faced hall dates back to the early part of the 17th century and is approached by a gatehouse erected by Roger Le Strange in around 1500. Behind at an angle are later 19th century additions comprising a north-west wing incorporating some 14th century walling. In the courtyard is a freestanding porch which was part of the Elizabethan house burnt in 1853. The later additions were affected by another fire in 1950. The Le Stranges sold off the hall in 1949, and what remains, is in three separate houses in different ownerships.

Between the Wars, Hunstanton Hall was regularly let and on a number of occasions, the author P.G. Wodehouse (Plum) stayed there, both as a guest of the Le Stranges and as a short-term tenant. He used it both as a setting and as an inspiration for some of his literary works. Charles Le Strange was a friend of Plum's wife, Ethel, and he invited them to stay in the summer of 1926. The Hall greatly appealed to Plum, *"It was a real-life Blandings Castle, the estate encompassing more than a thousand acres, which included a lake, a park, many gardens and a moat. Part of the original mansion, built in 1623, had been destroyed by fire in the early nineteenth century and rebuilt in Victorian style, the house was so large that at least two-thirds of it hadn't been lived in for almost a century. Plum*

West Front, after the recent fire.

spent much of the time on the moat, sitting in a punt with his typewriter on a small bedside table and wishing that he could settle down permanently in a place like this. And he watched in wonderment the way that life was lived there, regretting only that he couldn't use any of it in a story because no one would believe it. By this he meant such things as the late arrival of an unexpected guest because of car trouble-said guest arriving eventually at three o'clock in the morning to find that his host had roused the entire household and had a five-course dinner waiting for him". In 1927 the Wodehouses rented for the summer, and in 1928 'Money for Nothing' was published in which the hall was fictionalised.

Hunstanton Hall.

They again rented in 1929, and were also guests of the Le Stranges for Christmas – one bitter memory being, *"that he was forced to don the old white tie and tails every evening"*. The summer of 1933 again saw them at Hunstanton where Plum spent much of his time working on 'Right Ho Jeeves'.

Part of the estate incorporated what is now the seaside resort of New Hunstanton. This was initially developed by Henry Styleman Le Strange (1815-1862). He was the grandson of Nicholas Styleman of Snettisham who had married Armine, the elder daughter of Sir Nicholas Le Strange. The key to this development was the construction of the Lynn and Hunstanton Railway, the deputy chairman of the Railway Company being Henry L' Estrange Styleman Le Strange of Hunstanton Hall. The railway had reached the site of New Hunstanton by the summer of 1862 only for Henry to die suddenly in July of heart disease. His successor, Hamon Le Strange, oversaw the development of the new town until, by 1896, a town hall had been constructed and civic status was achieved.

KEN HILL

For Norfolk, Ken Hill is unusual on several counts – it was built as a result of money made in industry – it is built of carrstone, quarried a short distance away – it is in the 'Queen Anne revival' style – and it was built initially as a 'shooting box' (and soon attracted the Prince of Wales from nearby Sandringham). It only later became the family seat following the addition of a small wing.

Edward Green was a Yorkshire Ironmaster who had patented a device for recirculating waste heat from steam boilers, called the 'Green's Economiser'. As is often the case it was the next generation that most benefited and his son Edward (1831-1923) became MP for Wakefield, a Captain in the West Yorkshire Yeomanry and was created a baronet in 1886. He was very fond of country pursuits and had taken the lease of Heath Old Hall near Wakefield. There he employed Norwich architect and designer, Thomas Jeckyll, to make interior and exterior alterations and design furniture.

In 1877 Sir Edward bought the Snettisham Estate from the L'Estanges and Ken Hill was commenced in 1879. The architect was John J Stevenson who up until then had primarily been the designer of town

houses in London. Thomas Jeckyll would have been the natural choice as architect but, by this time, he had become increasingly mentally ill and died in 1881. Sir Edward had married Mary Lycett and later generations have added hers to the family name.

Sir Edward Stephen Lycett Green, the 4th baronet, died in 1996 and, in 1999, Savills offered the house with five acres for sale. Christies held a country house contents auction in the same year which included furniture, designs and letters by Thomas Jeckyll originally from Heath Old Hall. Earlier in 1997, Christies had sold from the house 'Love and the Maiden' by the Pre-Raphaelite artist John Spencer Stanhope (1829-1908). Stanhope's mother was the youngest daughter of Thomas Coke, Earl of Leicester.

KETTERINGHAM HALL

The Hall, Ketteringham J & S 616

The childhood home of England's shortest reigning 'monarch'; the lady of the manor who tried to rescue Marie Antoinette and the dauphin; the Victorian squire who crossed swords with his puritan vicar; the American air force during the second world war; a school and a college; a base for developing racing cars; and today, offices – can any country house have seen more strands of history?

The house dates back to Tudor times when the manor was held by the Heveninghams (who originated from the Suffolk village) who had inherited in the 1490s under the will of Sir Henry Grey – Lady Jane Grey, 'Queen' for nine days was reputed to have been born and brought up at the house which was probably rebuilt sometime in the 16th century. William Heveningham, who sat in judgement of Charles I, was sentenced to death, later commuted to life in prison, after the restoration and it was this that possibly led to the eventual sale to Edward Atkyns, the son and heir of Sir Edward Atkyns, Lord Chief Baron to the Exchequer.

It was Charlotte Atkyns (a Walpole of the Irish branch), actress and wife of a later Edward Atkyns (who had inherited from an uncle), who devoted her widowhood to trying to rescue the Queen of France from the prisons of the revolution, mortgaging the estate in the process and dying in Paris in penury in 1836. A tablet in Ketteringham Church states, *"Mrs*

Charlotte Atkyns, wife of Edward Atkyns Esq of Ketteringham, lies buried in an unknown grave at Paris. She was the friend of Marie Antoinette, and made several brave attempts to rescue her from prison, and after that Queen's death strove to help the Dauphin of France". Her story is told in the book 'Mrs Pimpernel Atkyns' by E.E.P. Tisdall, published by Jarrolds in 1965.

It was at that time that John Boileau purchased the estate. He was created a baronet at the coronation of Queen Victoria in 1838 and had been brought up at Tacolneston Hall which remained in the family until 1920. As an avid antiquary and archaeologist, he also purchased Burgh Castle, the Roman Fort. It was Sir John who in 1840 employed the architect Thomas Allason to remodel the hall in the Gothic style, and then from 1852 the Norwich architect and designer, Thomas Jeckyll to make further alterations and improvements. Jeckyll had from 1847 been engaged to embellish the grounds with garden buildings in the 'Picturesque' tradition, and had also rebuilt the Norwich lodge and in 1851 the Keeper's lodge. Sir John's difficult relationship with his vicar is chronicled in Owen Chadwick's book, 'Victorian Miniature', published in 1960.

The Boileau's tenure at the hall and estate ended in 1947, with the contents including the fine library being disposed of by means of a country house auction in the same year. During the war, Ketteringham Hall played its part being, from December 1943, the Headquarters of the

2nd Air Division of the United States Air Force with Hethel, close by, becoming the USAAF 389th Bomb Group air base, flying B24 Liberators. By 1950 the hall was used as a school and then as a college before being purchased in the 1960s by Colin Chapman for the headquarters of Lotus Cars. The Airfield, which had ceased operations by 1948, was in 1964 also sold to Lotus. The hall is now divided and occupied for multi-office use.

KIMBERLEY HALL

In his autobiography 'The Whim of the Wheel' published in 2001, the 4th Earl of Kimberley, Johnny Wodehouse (d 2002), tells of how at the age of 17 he came to inherit the large house at Kimberley as well as the estates there and in Cornwall, how the military occupied the hall during the war and of the work required to rectify 'the horrendous mess' in which it was left. He also tells of how his love for life and women eventually led to the sale, in 1958, of the Kimberley Estate with mansion house and parklands, home farm, houses, cottages, thirteen let farms and several smallholdings, in all 4,252 acres in 91 lots.

The manor was acquired by the Wodehouses probably around 1400, with the present house the third to be built. In the summer of 1578, Queen Elizabeth, on her progress from London to Norfolk, stayed at the fortified and moated 15th century Kimberley Tower, then a house of over twenty rooms for living and sleeping as well as the kitchen, armoury, brew house, granary and stables. The moat and foundations of this now demolished house can still to be seen in the park today.

Sir John Wodehouse, the 4th baronet, was responsible for bringing country house architect, William Talman, to Kimberley. He was paid £58 probably for a land survey which included, *"new house design'd to be built"*, a vast mansion much on the scale of Castle Howard. By 1712 the house, on the existing smaller design, was commenced but lacked the corner turrets. These were added between 1755 and 1759 by gentleman architect Thomas Prowse MP for Sir Armine Wodehouse the 5th baronet, with nearly £10,000 being expended on remodelling. He also employed Capability Brown in 1762 to lay out the park and lake. P.G. Wodehouse, the author, was a descendant of Sir Armine.

Sir John, the 6th baronet, was created Baron Wodehouse in 1797, and John, the 3rd baron, was created the 1st Earl of Kimberley in 1866 (the South African gold mining town was named after him). The Earl was a Liberal politician, foreign secretary, and at the time of his death in 1902, Liberal Leader in the House of Lords. Following the 1958 sale, the Wodehouses left Norfolk and since then the house has been owned by Mr Ronald Buxton.

LANGLEY HALL

Langley Hall is home to the private school of the same name which moved from St Giles in Norwich in 1946 (where the actor, the late Sir John Mills, was a pupil).

In the middle ages, the estate formed part of the lands of the Abbey of Langley, the ruins of which are close to the north bank of the Yare. At the dissolution, the manor was granted to a John Berney and it was a later member of the family, Richard Berney, who built the hall sometime before his death in 1737. This can be seen in John Wooton's painting 'The Beauchamp-Proctor Family and friends at Langley Park' dated 1749 and now in the Norwich Castle Museum. Berney may have overreached himself when building Langley, as he died in debt. A John Southgate, who valued his estates in 1737, reported, *"the new built mansion house and gardens which cost at least £5–6,000, I value the house as materials to be pulled down and sold off the premises as in fact it appears to me of no more worth"*.

The sale of Berneys estates was long drawn out but by April 1739 a London merchant, George Proctor, had taken possession but he only lived until 1744 when his nephew, William Beauchamp, inherited. By Royal Assent, William added the name Proctor, was created a baronet in 1745 and became MP for Middlesex in 1747.

At around this time the Norwich architect/builder Matthew Brettingham, who had overseen the building of Holkham, was employed to make alterations including adding the four corner towers, the corridors and wings. Superb rococo plasterwork was undertaken by Charles Stanley, bookcases designed by Thomas Chippendale and the ceiling of the first floor boudoir painted to a theme of 'music and entertainment' by Andieu de Clermont. These can all be seen by the public when the main rooms are open at the annual 'Daffodil Days'. Unfortunately you can no longer see the fine library chimneypiece by Sir Henry Cheere following its theft a few years ago.

Sir William died in 1773 and was succeeded by his son Sir Thomas Beauchamp-Proctor who built the north dining room. The estate continued to pass by succession (and in the process the surnames reversed to Proctor-Beauchamp) and on the death of Sir Reginald in 1912, his eldest daughter Mrs Barker-Hahlo inherited and was granted the name Beauchamp by Royal Licence. It was her son, Jocelyn, who granted the headmaster, John Jevons, a 21 year lease of the hall at £300 per annum in 1946 following its vacation by the army. Sighting death duties, he then

CHEDGRAVE LODGE, LANGLEY PARK.

sold the entire estate to Broadland Properties Ltd in April 1957. At that time it comprised 3,932 acres and produced £9,000 per annum. By June the purchaser had arranged an auction of over 100 lots which raised £153,127 with, at valuation, a further £25,916 unsold. The hall did not sell and was withdrawn at £7,500 (remarkably similar to the valuation of over 200 years previously) but was subsequently purchased by John Jevons with the school later becoming an educational trust.

The Lodges

Close to Loddon on the Norwich to Beccles road are two fine pairs of lodges which, with the dispersal of the estate, no longer really lead anywhere. They were designed in 1784 for Sir Thomas Beauchamp-Proctor by country house architect Sir John Soane but not completed until 1792. Soane's bill book refers to £26-5/- paid for, '2 *grey hound dogs as per agreement*' which can be seen in the photograph. Both lodges have been unused for many years but have been the subject of restoration in the second half of the 20th century.

LETTON HALL

In the 18th century, agriculture brought wealth to the County, and in the early years, Norwich was still England's second City. Some of the leading country house architects and interior designers of the day undertook commissions in Norfolk and the landscape gardeners, Capability Brown and Humphrey Repton, were engaged in laying out parks. One architect, whose life and work is commemorated in the museum created from his home, was John Soane (knighted in 1831).

Much of Soane's early work was undertaken for the gentry of Norfolk and Suffolk, and Letton Hall in 1783, for Brampton Gurdon Dillingham, was his first major country house commission. Gurdon, who had taken the surname Dillingham, wished to replace the old house (of which an engraving appears in volume VIII of Armstrong's History of Norfolk published in 1781) that he had inherited from his father, Thornhagh Gurdon. The basic square house as designed by Soane survives, but is compromised by later 19th century additions, however, the extensive offices court and stables remain. Soane made thirty-eight visits during the

Letton Hall.

course of its construction which, by 1792, had cost £6,000. Soanes's diligence is marked against some of his contemporaries, Wyatt for example tended to be tardy or, at times, totally absent.

The Gurdons remained until 1913 when the 2nd Lord Cranworth (the barony having had been created in 1899) put the 4,500 acre estate up for auction as a whole or in parts. It then comprised the hall, woodland and some thirty farms and smallholdings, all producing £4,908 per annum. The opening and only bid of £40,000 for the whole was refused and the subsequent 63 lot sale saw only 11 selling, producing £17,678. The hall remained unsold but was subsequently purchased by the Eglingtons who still farm part of the estate. The family sold the hall with ten acres in 1979 to a Mr Peter Carroll who runs it as a Christian Holiday and Activity Centre.

LEXHAM HALL

East Lexham Hall

The estate has been in the ownership of several noted county families throughout the centuries. Thomas L'Estrange succeeded at the time of Queen Elizabeth and it passed by marriage to the Wodehouses who built the present house. It was in the hands of Edmund Wodehouse in the early years of the 18th century followed by his nephew Sir John, the builder of Kimberley Hall, and then another John, the 1st Earl of Kimberley, who enlarged the house in 1780 but had sold by 1800. The Keppels came in 1806, making further alterations and extending, and they stayed until 1912 when Major Bertram Keppel sold to Augustus Leverton Jessop, nephew of the noted Norfolk antiquary Dr Augustus Jessop. A three day contents auction was held at the house in 1911.

The Jessop tenure lasted until the second world war after which it was acquired by the Fosters. William Foster employed the architect James Fletcher Watson, who designed the current Bawdeswell Church, to make internal and external improvements. He has also done much to create Lexham as 'a model village'. Lexham Hall is now the home of Mr and Mrs Neil Foster.

LYNFORD HALL

As with Ken Hill, Lynford was built as a result of money made in industry, though there the similarity ends. Jennifer Roberts' book published in 2003, 'Glass, The Strange History of the Lyne Stephens Fortune', tells the story of how William Stephens, born in 1731 as the illegitimate son of a Cornish servant girl, was to become one of the richest industrialists in Europe; in his genius opening a glass factory in Portugal, and eventually being granted a monopoly and exemption from paying taxes. It also tells of how his fortune passed to a young cousin, making him the richest commoner in England and husband of the infamous French ballerina Yolande.

That young cousin was Stephens Lyne Stephens – his portrait painted in 1858/9 shows an opulent man in his fifties with, in one hand, a wad of banknotes denoting his status as England's richest commoner. It was in 1851 that he inherited the fortune from his father which, in today's values, gave him an annual income of over two million pounds. He spent liberally, particularly with respect to property, and in 1856 he was made aware that the 8,000 acre estate with mansion house at Lynford was due to be auctioned. This he purchased for £133,500 but was not satisfied with the existing house which had been remodelled as recently as 1827. Country House architect William Burn had worked for him previously so was the obvious choice to design a brand new Jacobean style country house with fifty bedrooms and loosely based on Hatfield House which Stephens had admired from afar. Commenced in 1857, it cost an incredible £145,000 before its completion in 1861. Stephens, however, did not live to move into his grand house, dying in February 1860 at the age of 58. Clearly the excesses as a result of his inherited fortune had brought their own reward. Yolande, with a life's interest under her husband's will, moved into the hall in 1862 but remained a widow and was largely shunned by society. She died there in 1894.

Subsequently the estate changed hands several times until, in 1924, the then owner, a Captain Montagu, sold 6,200 acres to the forestry commission which was to form part of Thetford Forest. In 1928 the hall was gutted by fire, and two years later the forestry commission purchased and restored it, except the totally destroyed East Wing. The Commission let to the Scottish distiller and timber merchant, Sir James Calder, as a grace and favour residence. He was a friend of Joseph Kennedy, and entertained him and his son, JFK, at Lynford. Calder had purchased the nearby Weeting Hall estate in 1917, primarily for the timber, and sold the major portion to the Forestry Commission in 1925. During the second world war, Lynford was used as an officers' convalescent hospital and, afterwards, as a training college for foresters. The hall became increasingly run-down and was privately purchased in 1971 and restored. It has since been used as an hotel and conference centre.

MANNINGTON HALL

Mannington Hall near Aylsham

It is a rarity for a 15th century house to survive in anything like its original form and only three in Norfolk come quickly to mind: Elsing, Oxborough with the third being Mannington; all are moated.

A friend of the Pastons, a William Lumnor wrote to John Paston in 1460, *"I am building a poor house, I trust God you shall take your lodgings there when you come to your lordships in these parts"*. He had been granted a licence to crenellate in 1451 and Mannington was probably somewhere near to completion by 1460 which was at the time of the Wars of the Roses. Subsequently the house passed through related families until in 1736, on the death of Mary the second wife of Sir Charles Potts, it was sold for a reported £20,000 to Horatio Walpole.

Horatio, later the 1st Baron Walpole, was the brother of Robert Walpole, Britain's first prime minister, and was engaged on the building of his fine new house nearby at Wolterton. It is probable that he wished to extend his estates and only meant for Mannington to be used as dower house or farmhouse. It was this very lack of status that was the key to its survival unaltered. It was not until Horatio's great great grandson, the 4th Earl of Orford (of the second creation), inherited in 1858 that it was to become the family seat. An antiquarian and lover of gothic, he abandoned Wolterton, made Mannington his home and made alterations and additions including, as did his brother Frederick at Rainthorpe, embellishing with architectural features from other houses. Robert, the 5th and last earl, resided there from 1895 to 1905 after which he returned to Wolterton which he had restored.

Mannington was again let, with one tenant, Sir Charles Tomes, writing a book in 1916 entitled 'Mannington Hall and its owners'. Lady Dorothy Nevill, the sister of the 4th earl, also wrote about, and photographed, the house for her book 'Mannington and the Walpoles'. The present Lord Walpole returned to live there in 1969. The gardens and grounds are open to the public as is the house on occasion.

MELTON CONSTABLE HALL

MELTON CONSTABLE HALL,

Though architecturally one of the major houses of its style in Britain, the last 60 years have seen episodes of emptiness, neglect, dry rot, decay and repair notices which, even with a reluctant sale, have yet to be determined.

The estate came to the Astleys in 1236 as a result of the marriage between Sir Thomas Astley kt, and Editha, the co-heir of Sir Robert Constable, and they held it continuously for over 700 years until the cycle of neglect commenced in the late 1940s. The builder of the house was Jacob Astley, a royalist commander during the civil war and who was made a baronet after the restoration in 1660. He probably considered the Elizabethan house that he had inherited from his uncle old-fashioned and, only retaining one side as servants' quarters, he set about building the new 9 x 7 bay house which comprises the main part that stands today. It was probably completed by about 1687 as one of the fine plaster ceilings is so dated. There is no documentary evidence as to the architect of such an important house though William Samwell, who worked at Felbrigg, has been suggested. Its importance was emphasised by being the only Norfolk house to be engraved for the two massive early 18th century architectural works by Samuel and Nathaniel Buck, and by Johannes Kip.

In 1763/4 Capability Brown drew up plans for the deer park which took five years to complete at a cost of £2,500, and also provided drawings for a temple, aviary and gothic summerhouse. Major alterations and additions were undertaken in 1812 when the main block was joined to the Elizabethan service wing, with further additions in the late 19th and early 20th centuries. In his book 'Astleys of Melton Constable 1236 to 1936', Sir Delaval Astley (the 21st Baron Hastings) gives a picture of life at Melton Constable through the centuries including when, in 1841, Sir Jacob, the 6th baronet, succeeded in having the barony of Hastings called

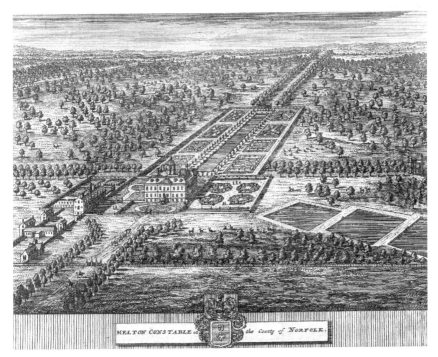

MELTON CONSTABLE in the County of NORFOLK.

out of abeyance. He also tells of the sporting prowess of Sir George, the
20th Baron and how he maintained a stud on the estate, and in 1885, won
the Derby with his horse Melton ridden by Fred Archer.

His successor, Sir Delaval, inherited in 1904 and has been described as
more of a man of the 19th rather than the 20th century. He inherited a
heavily mortgaged estate but kept it largely intact, only selling East
Barsham in 1914 and part of that at Snoring in the 1930s. Pre-War days
were still grand with an inside staff approaching twenty. Possibly affected
by the post war political changes, Sir Delaval saw no future for estates
with great country houses and gave the Northumberland Seaton Delaval
Estate to his eldest son (which included Vanbrugh's great house),
negotiated the sale of the Melton estate to the trustees of the Duke of
Westminster, and moved to Swanton House nearby.

From this time, it was a downward spiral. The Grosvenor Estates
auctioned all the contents, including reportedly the Chinese wallpaper
from the walls, and let unfurnished. They then sold the estate in 1959 to
a Mr G.W. Harold who farmed but had no interest in the house, leaving it
empty. Despite cosmetic improvements carried out when it was used as
the setting for the film 'The Go Between', the house rapidly deteriorated.
In 1983, and under pressure from preservation authorities and in failing
health, Mr Harold put the house and estate on the market but later
withdrew it. It then comprised 2,200 acres including the 200 acre grounds
and deer park, the 17 acre lake, lodges, the Dairy farm, coach house and

stables, farmhouses and cottages, estate yard, stud farm, sawmill and blacksmiths, water tower and the historic Bath house (seen in the engravings and later subject of improvement by Capability Brown). By the late 1980s Roger Gawn had purchased the house and surrounding land and has commenced some restoration work, though the future is yet uncertain.

MERTON HALL

The estate was inherited by the De Greys in the 1330s and they have lived here ever since. The 'E' plan house was built by 1613, probably on the footprint of an earlier hall, with the detached gatehouse completed seven years later. The gothic revival architect, Edward Blore, attended Merton twice in the 19th century. In 1831 he reported to Lord Walsingham (the barony was created in 1780), *"the whole of the interior and the roof is in a state of absolute decay"*. The house had been unoccupied since 1781, and between 1832 and 1837 Blore carried out work costing £5,926 with a further £2,964 expended between 1846 and 1848. The result was a thorough restoration of the existing house, a neo-Jacobean service wing in the existing style, and a further room beyond the west wing.

It may be said that Merton is notable for two things – Sport and Bad luck!

In the time of the Victorian 6th baron, not only was the estate famous for its shooting which attracted royalty and the Prince of Wales in particular, but the Baron himself vied with Lord Ripon as to who was the greatest shot of the time. He made history by killing 1070 grouse in one day on Blubberhouse Moor at the rate of nearly two birds each minute, but only fired 1,510 cartridges. He was also a scientist, a keen ornithologist, an entomologist, and with Payne-Gallwey, penned the two shooting volumes in the Badminton Library series of sporting books. His brother, the 7th baron, was also a noted sportsman but counted fishing equal to shooting. He wrote two small books – 'Fish' in 1926 and 'Hit and Miss' in the following year.

Bad luck came in several guises. The scourge of the country house is fire, and after the second world war the house was let to a school, with the family living nearby in a modern house. In 1956 fire gutted the original 17th century block, only sparing the Blore wing. Another fire, in 1970, destroyed the modern house leading the present owner, the 9th baron, to return to the Blore wing.

Bad luck or bad judgement blighted the last years of the sporting 6th baron. Rich when he came into the 12,000 acre Merton estate and with two further estates in Yorkshire soon to be inherited, his hospitality and the lavish manner in which he led his life were legion. The Prince of Wales alone was a drain on any estate (as he had been at Gunton) and it is said that in the 1890s, in one year, he exhausted the Merton wine cellar that had been built up over generations. Baron Walsingham also lost a reported one million pounds in a London speculation whereby he demolished Walsingham House, now the site of the Ritz, to replace it with a (failed) residential club. The Yorkshire estates and London property had to be sold as well as outlying portions of the Merton estate. Fortunately Merton itself was entailed. He died abroad in 1919.

The third piece of bad luck was as a result of the second world war when a greater part of the estate was taken by the war department to create the Battle Area. Rather than release the land at cessation of hostilities as promised, a compulsory purchase order was made for 7,500 acres at £25 per acre! Today, Merton still has its shoot which is now let and extends to about 3,700 acres.

MIDDLETON TOWER

The 1812 and 1817 etchings by John Sell Cotman, and the mid 18th century engraved drawing by Millicent, show a ruinous brick tower with lower remains to the west side. Was this all that was left of a vast fortified house of the date and style of Oxburgh, or the brick remains of a smaller timber framed house? Neither Cotman or Millicent show a moat, though there certainly had been, as there is now.

The manor was in the hands of the de Scales at least by the 12th century and it seems that it was Thomas, the 7th Lord Scales, who was responsible for building the gatehouse. Born just before 1400, he was a prominent figure of his time. He was awarded with an annuity of £100 for life for services in the French wars to Henrys V and VI. He was murdered in London in 1460

Middleton Castle Norfolk.

London Published by Cooper Hood & Sharpe, Poultry, July 1, 1819.

whilst fighting for the Lancastrian cause and his estate was inherited by his daughter Elizabeth who became Baroness Scales.

Subsequently, the Manor passed through many hands. In 1854 the Middleton Estate was put up for auction comprising a gentlemanly residence called Middleton Cottage, Blackborough Priory founded in the reign of Henry 2nd, and the Tower or Ruin of the Castle of Middleton, all within 2,823 acres. By 1856, a Kings Lynn banker, Sir Lewis Whincorp Jarvis, was the owner and set about restoring the gatehouse and extending to the west. After his death in 1888 the house was let but in the early 20th century it was acquired by a John Taylor Ramsden who was responsible for adding further rooms and much of the panelling. Following the death of his son, Thomas, in 1960 Middleton Tower passed by inheritance to his granddaughter, Mrs Timothy Barclay.

NARFORD HALL

It seems that the Fountaines came to Narford from Salle in 1690 when Andrew Fountaine purchased the estate. In a memorandum, preserved at the hall and in his own hand, is written, *"1702 Monday 29th June I laid the first stone of my house at Narford"*. An engraving of this house, before the later extensive alterations, can be seen in 'Views of the Seats of Noblemen and Gentlemen' by J.P. Neale which was published from 1818.

His eldest son was the notable virtuoso, Sir Andrew Fountaine, who was knighted in 1698 and, in 1727, succeeded Sir Isaac Newton as Warden of the Mint. He travelled extensively in Europe during the opening years of the 18th century only to be called back to Narford late in 1703, possibly because of his father's failing health. After his father's death in 1706, he preferred to stay in London and let Narford. He undertook a second 'Grand Tour' from 1714 and amassed, by purchase at both home and abroad, a remarkable collection of pictures, statuary, antiquities, coins, books and in particular a collection of majolica and Limoges enamels. Andieu de Clermont (see Langley) was commissioned to paint ceilings and the house was adorned with inset canvases by the Venetian artist Giovanni Antonio Pellegrini (1675-1741). Sir Andrew finally left his house in St James Place for Narford in the early 1730s, reportedly living a rather solitary existence until his death twenty years later.

NARFORD LAKE.

Alterations and additions continued to be made to the house until, in about 1860, substantial additions were made which included a four storey domed tower, a new porch and a two storey three bay carrstone wing with a tiny attic storey over a square projecting bay. William Burn, the Victorian country house architect who designed Lynford, has been given responsibility but this is by no means certain. Narford, along with Holkham, Houghton, Blickling, Raynham and Wolterton, was in the top rank of visited houses by the gentry when undertaking their 'Norfolk Tours' of country houses and their parks.

Successive Fountaines followed the example of Sir Andrew and were bitten with the collecting bug, but in June 1884, Christies held a famous four day auction of majolica, Limoge enamels and other antiquities removed from Narford. This was followed, in July 1886, with a sale of engravings and old master drawings.

The late owner, Commander Andrew Fountaine who died in 1997, was a founder of the National Front and was a kinsman of Margaret Fountaine, the butterfly lady, who left her collections to the Castle Museum. The books 'Love among the Butterflies' and 'Butterflies and Late Loves' are based on her diaries which were dramatically revealed when, 100 years after her birth, a japanned metal box was opened under her written instructions in 1978.

OXBURGH HALL

The Bedingfields, who came to Oxburgh in the early 15th century from the Suffolk village that bears their family name, were much in evidence in the history of the Tudor period. Sir Edmund Bedingfield, who was knighted at the coronation of Richard III, was given a licence to crenellate in July 1482 and built the great moated brick fortified house dominated by its massive gatehouse flanked by two projecting octagonal towers.

Henry VII with his Queen, Elizabeth of York, stayed here in 1487 with the room above the gateway in which he slept, now being named the King's Room. Sir Edmund died in 1496 and was survived by four sons, and the eldest, Thomas, attended Henry VIII's coronation in 1509 and was created a Knight of the Bath. He was succeeded by his brother Robert in 1539 and a year later by Edmund who had been knighted in 1523. It was this Sir Edmund who was much in favour with Henry VIII, being entrusted with the custody, and later the funeral, of Catherine of Aragon at the time she was being supplanted by Anne Boleyn. He died in 1554 and was succeeded by his eldest son Sir Henry who, being staunchly catholic, was a great supporter of Queen Mary and came to her assistance whilst she was in refuge at Framlingham Castle at the time that Lady Jane Grey made claim to the throne. After Mary's accession she made him Knight Marshall of the Army, Captain of the Guard and Governor of the Tower of London. Her sister, Elizabeth, was placed under his custody both at the Tower and at Woodstock. Initially after Elizabeth's accession in 1558, it appears that he was born little ill will, and Oxburgh was intended as a stopover in her 'Progress' to Norfolk in 1578. However, at the time, whilst at Woodrising nearby, Sir Henry was examined as a recusant and, on refusing to conform, he was placed under house arrest at Norwich. Ill health eventually allowed his return to Oxburgh where he died in 1583.

During the Civil War, the Bedingfields espoused the royalist cause and, in a County conspicuous for its allegiance to Cromwell, suffered for it. Land was forcibly sold or confiscated and the house pillaged and part burnt. Reportedly nearly £50,000 was lost in the cause of the King. On the accession of the monarchy, rather than financial restitution, Charles II granted a baronetcy in 1661 to Henry, the great grandson of the Tudor Henry.

Today, the Bedingfields still live at Oxburgh, but only just! For financial reasons Sir Edmund Bedingfield, the 9th and present baronet, sold the estate in 1952 to property developers only for them to reoffer the house for sale. This the Dowager Lady Bedingfield (Sybil Lyne-Stephens), with help from others, took the opportunity to repurchase and give to the National Trust with the proviso that it should remain the Bedingfield home. On a more recent note, in 2004, the Trust was able to purchase for £20,000 items that had left the hall in a 1951 sale. These were offered by Bonhams at the auction sale of the contents of Banningham rectory, the home of Bryan Hall. He, with his father, had attended the Norfolk country house contents dispersals that had been so prevalent in the decades following the second world war including, presumably, that of Oxburgh.

PICKENHAM HALL

A lithograph published in the mid 19th century shows a long low two storey rendered house with pilasters and magnificent Greek Ionic portico, designed by W.J. Donthorne circa 1829 for William Lyde Wiggett-Chute. He lived at the 'The Vyne', a classical house in Hampshire (bequeathed by a successor to the National Trust in 1956), and sold Pickenham soon after. By the opening years of the 20th century perhaps this was thought old-fashioned or was it in poor condition? Whichever, it was largely swept away in 1902 when the banker G.W. Taylor, who had reportedly inherited a fortune from button making in Moseley, purchased the estate. He commissioned the arts and crafts architect Robert Weir Schultz, a

W. Gould & Son's Series.   Pickenham Hall.

Scotsman and contemporary of Mackintosh, to design a new house much in the style of the day. Little of the old house was saved – a few walls and the library – but by 1905, at a cost of over £20,000, the house that stands today was complete.

In 1924 it was acquired by J.S. Moreton whose family were in residence until 1986 when it was sold, lock stock and barrel, for in excess of five million pounds to Richard Daniels, a self-made man, who had started out 30 years previously by making garden sheds. It was reported that he saw the advert for the estate in Country Life, sent for the details, liked it and purchased. He had never previously visited Norfolk. The estate comprised 3,500 acres, 3 farms, 2 miles of the river Wissey and almost the entire village of Pickenham. The estate was again for sale in 1993.

QUIDENHAM HALL

Two families were particularly associated with Quidenham. The first was the Hollands, prominent parliamentarians, who owned from the 1570s to the 1740s, with the male line having died out in 1729. Little remains of the house they built though we know its style from a fine architects model now at the museum of Norfolk life at Gressenhall. The other family was the Keppels, noted for their military and naval exploits, who purchased in 1762.

The Keppels came over from Holland with William of Orange, and Arnold Joost van Keppel, evidently a brilliant and courageous soldier, was created the first Earl of Albemarle in 1696. The 2nd earl served in both the Foot and Horse Guards and rose to the rank of Lieutenant-General. He had four children (in reverse order) – Frederick the Bishop of Exeter, Sir William a general, Augustus an admiral and 1st Lord of the Admiralty (created Viscount Keppel) and George a lieutenant-general and the 3rd earl, who succeeded in 1754. George was CinC at the campaign which saw the fall of Havana in 1762 and with his prize of £120,000, purchased the estate at Quidenham from a John Bristow who had built the East wing. The expedition to Havana was quite a family affair with Augustus as commodore of the fleet (his prize money went towards the purchase of the estate at Elveden near Thetford), and William, then a brigadier, 2nd in command to his brother.

THE HALL, QUIDENHAM.

Under the Keppels the house was to see many alterations and extensions into the late 1880s. Many trophies and souvenirs of service on land and sea were on display. Both the 5th and 6th Earls were at Waterloo and Henry, their brother, was Admiral of the Fleet Sir Henry Keppel whose biography 'The Beloved Little Admiral' by Vivian Stuart was published in 1967. Two other Keppels can be mentioned: Alice Keppel, daughter of George the third son of the 7th earl, was the mistress of King Edward VII, and Judith Keppel, the first million pound winner in the TV programme, who is a distant relation.

The 9th earl was the last to live at Quidenham, departing for Suffolk in 1948, when the house became a Carmelite Convent which it remains today.

RACKHEATH HALL

I have on my wall at home a large framed lithograph, by Hobday & Roberts of Cheapside, which shows a handsome white brick mansion in the italianate style entitled 'Rackheath Hall The Seat of Henry Stracey Esq.'. The house stands in manicured gardens and faces parkland with woods beyond. Sir Henry Josias Stracey, the 5th baronet, inherited the title in 1855 so the lithograph must date from a few years before. It took barely 100 years for this idyllic scene to be replaced by one of neglect, misfortune, vandalism and despair, which surprisingly seems to have run its course but not with demolition, as with so many, but with a new chapter.

The estate was purchased in 1773 from the Pettus family by Edward Stracey (he was created a baronet in 1818 and died in 1829) who it seems was responsible for the present hall, which was then remodelled in about 1850. Perhaps this is the reason for, and is contemporary with, my lithograph. The Straceys were a typical County family. Several became High Sheriffs and Sir Henry was an MP for East Norfolk, Yarmouth and Norwich. It is said that Lloyd George offered a successor, Sir Edward Paulet Stracey, an earldom for £30,000, but he was reportedly quite content with his baronetcy. It was following the death of Sir Edward in 1949 that the Stracey tenure at Rackheath came to a close. The USAF 467th Bombardment Group had occupied the park and house during the closing years of the war, and perhaps it was the aftermath of this that led, in 1950, to the auctioning of the 1,500 acre estate including the hall, 7 farms, 29 cottages and woodland all in 48 lots. The lots that sold fetched £62,000, but the hall with 4 acres did not fetch a bid.

Not long after, Sydney Cranmer, an antiques dealer, purchased the hall for use as a showroom and warehouse which he ran for 30 years. Rackheath then remained empty for nearly 20 years becoming desolate and prey of thieves and vandals. It was sold at the height of the property boom in 1988 for £530,000 to a Mr Karrar who hoped to gain planning permission for flats and to resell for a vast profit. Following his financial demise, it was on the market in 1990 for £300,000 selling for £80,000 less in the following year, but this time with the planning approval. Again it was for sale in 1997 for £325,000, and now has been successfully converted by London developer, George Braithwaite, into flats with houses built sympathetically in the grounds.

RAINTHORPE HALL

Seemingly an 'E' plan Elizabethan house with half timbering to the first floor, but in fact a house which exhibits the tastes of successive owners. A local barrister, Thomas Baxter, acquired the manor in 1579 and virtually rebuilt the house – the 'E' plan north front, the Great Hall and the octagonal stair turret being survivors of this era. Thomas died in 1611 and after the family sold in 1628, Rainthorpe passed through many hands until it was purchased in 1852 by the Honourable Frederick Walpole.

Frederick was a younger son of the 3rd earl of Orford (of Wolterton and Mannington), MP for North Norfolk and had a keen appreciation for history. He introduced panelling, some of the fireplaces and spent a great deal of money on embellishing the house in an antiquarian style. Following Walpole's death in 1876 another antiquarian, Sir Charles Harvey Bt, purchased and built a 5 bay wing at the west end of the south front and at right angles to it. He also added further panelling and stained glass.

The Harveys sold in 1934 to J. Maurice Hastings who had married an American bank note heiress, and he further restored the interior in the Elizabethan style. He was succeeded by his son George Hastings, a barrister, musician and friend of Dudley Moore who, following his divorce, lived there alone. He and Rainthorpe were the subject of a chapter in John Young's book 'The Country House in the 1980s' which

was published in 1981. Following his early death in 1993, the contents were auctioned by Sothebys, and the house with 16 acres was sold for £614,000 in the autumn of 1994 to Alastair and Suzy Wilson.

RAVENINGHAM HALL

The estate, within which this fine Georgian house stands, is some 4,000 acres and has been in the Bacon family since 1713 when Sir Edmund Bacon, the 4th Redgrave baronet, married Mary Castell whose family had lived here since the 13th century. The Bacon baronets can be rather confusing and I have included a few lines of explanation in the entry for Gillingham Hall, however, another Sir Edmund (8th/9th) built this house on an undeveloped site in about 1750. In the late 19th/early 20th century, Captain Nicholas Bacon (later 12th/13th) added the portico to the south front, the two storey wings to each side (subsequently demolished by his son), dormers to the attics, an extension to the rear on the north side, and alterations to the interior.

The 'father' of the family was Nicholas Bacon, the great lawyer and Keeper of the Privy Seal who was knighted by Queen Elizabeth in 1558. He clearly had the benefit of wisdom and, as a protestant, felt able to

support the catholic Mary in her claim to the throne. He thrived under Elizabeth and when he entertained her at his house at Redgrave in Suffolk she remarked, *'My Lord, what a little house you have gotten'*, his reply being, *'Madam, my house is well, but it is you who have made me too great for my house'*. It was his eldest son, also Nicholas, who inherited Redgrave and in 1611 was created the first ever baronet by James 1st – who charged £1095 for the honour.

The third son of this Sir Nicholas Bt, Butts, was also created a baronet in 1627 (of Mildenhall). In 1755 Richard, the 8th Mildenhall baronet, succeeded to the Redgrave title so becoming 7th of Redgrave and 8th of Mildenhall. The Bacons remain the premier baronets of the country but also retain this additional title. The present incumbent, who inherited in 1982, is Sir Nicholas (14th/15th).

Donald Lindsay's book, 'Sir Edmund Bacon A Norfolk Life', published in 1988, not only details the life of Sir Edmund throughout the 20th century, but also gives much background history of the Bacon family.

RAYNHAM HALL

The Townshends have been at Raynham since the 14th century and fragments of their former house are still present within cottages near to the lake. The story of the great house that stands today begins with Sir Roger Townshend, the first baronet (created in 1617), who inherited in 1603 at the age of about seven from his father who had been killed in a duel. It had always been generally believed that Raynham was built from designs by Inigo Jones, but with no records or evidence that Jones ever visited, this theory has in recent times been discounted. What is known is that Sir Roger had licence to travel abroad in 1620-22 when it is believed he visited Venice and Tuscany, and also the Netherlands where he was accompanied by his mason William Edge. It is possible also that he had seen drawings by Jones, as those for the Prince's Lodging at Newmarket were being executed in 1619.

What is known is that records held at the Hall dated August 30th 1619 note, *"This weeke Beginne the Building"*, and these continue until April 1620. However, this work was halted and discarded by the spring of 1621 as stone from the nearby dissolved Coxford Abbey had been used for the foundations. Evidently settlement had occurred, but the dread of the curse of sacrilege also probably played a part in determining its abandonment and recommencement a short distance away. It is unclear how complete the house was when Sir Roger died in 1637, though Sir Henry Spelman wrote in 1632, *"Sir Roger . . . hath there finished a stately house, using none of the Abbey stone about it"*. The inventory made at the time of Sir Roger's death indicate that it was not yet ready for occupation. He was succeeded by his son another Sir Roger and then, in about 1648, by Roger's brother Sir Horatio.

Sir Horatio was a royalist and had been sent to the tower for his part in the plot to seize Lynn for the King. On the restoration of the monarchy, he was honoured by Charles II who in 1661 created him Baron Townshend of Lynn Regis and in 1682 Viscount Townshend of Raynham. Charles visited Raynham in 1671 when the house must have appeared the finest in the County and most likely made Blickling and Melton Constable appear old fashioned. Horatio died in 1687 and was succeeded by his son Charles, the second viscount. He was the famous 'Turnip Townshend', the agricultural innovator, but foremost he was a politician becoming Secretary of State, Lord President of the Council and joint Ambassador at the Hague. His brother-in-law was Sir Robert Walpole, the first Prime-Minister, who at that time was planning his great house nearby at Houghton and which was to overshadow Raynham. It was during the 2nd Viscount's time that William Kent was engaged to remodel and decorate the interior, perhaps (unsuccessfully) in an attempt to rival Houghton. Legend says that the ghost of Dorothy Walpole, Charles' second wife, is the 'Brown Lady' that haunts both Raynham and Houghton.

George, the fourth Viscount, was a Field-Marshall and third in command at the siege of Quebec that saw the death of General Wolfe, and the Marquis de Montcalm which lead to the capitulation of the French. He was created a Marquess in 1787 and died in 1807. The seventh and present Marquess was, for twenty-seven years, the chairman of Anglia Television. The house, though formerly open to the public, is now a private family home.

RIDDLESWORTH HALL

The estate with its Elizabethan house (of which a watercolour survives) was in the ownership of the Drurys until sold in 1789 by their descendants to the Bevans. Sylvanus Bevan, a banker, had become very rich and had homes in London and Brighton as well as owning a number of country houses, Riddlesworth being one. His uncle was James Barclay of the banking family and, until 1993, Bevans still remained as directors of Barclays Bank. Following his purchase Sylvanus set about improving his estate, demolishing the 200 year old house and, by 1792, replacing it with the italianate building that is illustrated in 'Neales Seats'.

In 1814 he sold Riddlesworth to Thomas Thornhill whose successors sold in 1893 to W.N.L. Champion. Champion had been born in Edale in Derbyshire where he had inherited a sizeable estate which included the Blue John mine. He also owned textile mills in Lancashire and a brewery and coal mine in Yorkshire. At the time the 2,500 acre Riddlesworth estate was reported to be one of the finest sporting estates in Norfolk, and Champion undertook many improvements both to the estate and to the house. However, within six years it had been totally destroyed by fire. In those days fire was an ever present threat to large isolated country houses, only the largest having their own fire engines. The brigade, which had been established at Thetford in 1880, received a message via horseback that the hall was alight. Messengers were sent to the houses of the firemen and horses harnessed to the fire engine. By the time they reached the house it was strongly ablaze and efforts were concentrated on saving the adjoining offices and buildings, much of the contents having already been removed by the owner, servants and estate workers. By 1900 a new larger and more up to date house had been constructed, the architects being the Norwich firm of H.J. Green.

1939 saw both the death of W.N.L. Champion and of course the 2nd World War when the hall was used initially for evacuees and, from 1944, as a new home for Felixstowe College school. After the war this use continued and in 1983 the Allied Schools Group purchased it from a Mrs Noel who was the great grand-daughter of the late owner. It remains a school today. The late Diana Princess of Wales was a pupil for two years from the age of nine in 1970.

RYSTON HALL

It is ironic that Sir Roger Pratt was responsible for the design of a handful of the most important post restoration houses in the country, yet Ryston, which he designed for himself, has since been altered almost out of recognition.

Sir Roger, knighted by Charles II in 1668, was one of his commissioners for the rebuilding of London after the Great Fire. Of the houses that he designed – Kingston Lacy, Coleshill, Horseheath and Clarendon House in Piccadilly – apart from the first named which is in the hands of the National Trust, all have perished. Coleshill by fire in 1952 and Horseheath (1777) and Clarendon House (1683) both demolished, in fact Clarendon House, despite being one of the most influential domestic buildings in the history of English architecture, lasted a mere 16 years. It is fortunate that his notebooks with much detail of his designs still survive with the family, particularly since the houses had in the past generally been attributed to others.

The Pratts have been at Ryston since the 1500s and (Sir) Roger inherited the estate from his cousin in 1667 and by April 1669 had commenced the rebuilding of the hall. His notebooks tell us that by March 1672 work was apparently complete with an expenditure of £2,880. 7/7d. Ryston was Sir Roger's last work after which it seems he took up the life of a country gentleman. It is fortunate that a contemporary watercolour of

South Front, Ryston Hall

the house remains at the hall as by the last decade of the 18th century its appearance had been vastly altered.

In 1786 Edward Pratt, who had inherited the estate two years before and married a Kings Lynn heiress, engaged John Soane, whom he had met on his grand tour, to remodel the 1670s house. By 1794 £3,704 had been spent the result being a thoroughly updated house at a far cheaper cost than starting afresh. Soane illustrated the plans in his major architectural work, 'Plans, Elevations, and Sections of Buildings', which he had published in 1788.

Anthony Salvin undertook internal alterations in 1864 for the Reverend Jermyn Pratt, and just before the first World War, further alterations were made for Edward Roger Murray Pratt including the construction of a three bay mansard roof with dormers to each front, and the joining of the house to the pavilions with two storey additions. Ryston is now the seat of Piers Pratt who farms the 3,000 acre estate.

SALLE PARK

Salle Park (pronounced Saul) is a typically Georgian red brick house of two storeys and 7 bays with 2 small wings. It was built by Edward Hase, who was the brother of Sir John Lombe (formerly Hase) Bt of Bylaugh, and was commenced in early 1763 with the family moving in on October 15th 1765. Medium sized country houses of that period could be built for a relatively modest amount and Salle cost £2,470 with a further £565 for the walls of the kitchen garden. Edward Hase's eldest daughter, Virtue, had married Richard Paul Jodrell and from her the Jodrells inherited the Lombe baronetcy through the female line.

The Jodrells owned Salle until 1890 when the estate was acquired by Timothy White. On his death in 1908, it passed to a son (Sir) Woolmer who was created a baronet in 1922. It is now the seat of Sir John Woolmer White, the 4th baronet, who farms the award winning 4,000 acre estate.

Further information about the Jodrells and Salle can be found in volume 4 of 'Heraldry in Norfolk Churches' where R.C. Fiske has contributed a detailed note.

SANDRINGHAM

7049   SANDRINGHAM HOUSE.

The choice of Sandringham as the home for the future King must have been for reasons other than for the architecture of the house that then stood. This had substantially replaced an earlier house, was completed by the early 1770s and stood in an estate of over 5,000 acres. The house was ungainly in appearance and apparently inconveniently arranged for the Prince, for whom sport and entertaining were predominant. Arthur Young, the agriculturist, described the estate, *"as considerable tracts of sandy land suitable for the feeding of rabbits and incapable of cultivation but suitable for plantations which thrive extremely"*. The house was built for Cornish Hoste Henley who was succeeded by his son, Henry Hoste Henley, soon after when he was only seven years of age. Henry's four children predeceased him so, a year or two after his death in 1833, the estate was put up for auction. The auction catalogue described a mansion suitable for a family of the first respectability within a deer park and pleasure grounds with plantations and approached by a carriage drive through avenues of trees. The park, enclosed within a stone wall and paling, commanded views of the adjacent country, and within the domain of 5,450 acres which included the entire parishes of Sandringham, Babingley and Wolferton. It was purchased for £76,000 by John Motteux from Beachamwell Hall who did not live there but increased the size of the estate to 7,000 acres. He was a bachelor and in his will Sandringham was to pass to Charles Spencer Cowper, the third son of his late friend Earl Cowper the stepson of Lord Palmerston and then Foreign Minister. Evidently the second son was the designated heir until he married (a Gurney) only weeks before Motteux's death. Cowper took possession in 1843 and in the 1850s he employed the High Victorian architect, S.S. Teulon, to design new chimneys and build an extravagantly decorated entrance porch and conservatory.

By 1861 Prince Albert, the Prince Consort, was on the look-out for a country home for his son Albert Edward, the Prince of Wales. Under consideration, among others, were Newstead Abbey, former home of Byron, Somerleyton in Suffolk and Lynford Hall in Breckland. Walpole's great Houghton Hall stood empty but perhaps was considered too grand. It is not clear why Sandringham was chosen though it was private, in easy travelling distance of London by rail and within a county where there were respected families who could provide social and sporting contacts. Also, being owned by the then Prime Minister's stepson, its availability would have been made known. Following inspection in February 1862, minds were made up and it was purchased for £220,000, nearly three times the amount it had fetched at auction 26 years before.

With little delay the Prince began improvements to the estate. He employed the architect A.J. Humbert to build cottages, lodges, accommodation for staff and Park House for his comptroller as well as Bachelors' Cottage beyond the lake (now called York House). He also built a model farm, stud and gamestore and constructed a new garden wall in which were accommodated the Norwich gates, designed by Thomas Jeckyll for the 1862 Great Exhibition, which were a wedding present from the County and City.

Humbert, who had converted Teulon's conservatory into a billiard room, provided plans for extending and embellishing the existing hall which were not carried out. However, by 1867, the Prince had outgrown Sandringham and spent Christmas at Park House with Humbert having been given instructions to demolish the hall but to keep Teulon's chimneys and conservatory (with a matching bowling alley in the same style to be built alongside) for incorporation in a new house. The Christmas of 1869 was spent at Gunton but by the following year the new house was just about ready. It was reported to be, *"Quite charming, a very great improvement on the old one, and nicely furnished. It is warm and very comfortable and feels quite dry"*. The most modern sanitary installations were introduced under the supervision of Thomas Crapper.

The Queen made her first visit in 1871 to attend to the Prince whilst he was suffering from a serious attack of typhoid fever. On his recovery he

continued to delight in improving and showing off his estate. In 1877 a new water tower, standing 121 feet above Sandringham and holding 32,000 gallons, was built at Appleton and by 1884 the house had a new ballroom, with a large adjoining conservatory added in 1887. A serious fire to the upper floors in 1891 resulted in additional bedrooms being constructed above the billiard room and bowling alley. Edward's elder son, the Duke of Clarence, died of influenza in January 1892 and his brother Prince George, the eventual heir and engaged to Mary, set up home at Bachelors Cottage. After Edward became King in 1901 he spent far less time at Sandringham though Alexandra continued to do so in the company of her son nearby and her youngest daughter at Appleton House, which had been built in 1863 for Edward's farm tenant Louisa Cresswell. Louisa was a forthright person who was happy to make her opinions known and was quite a thorn in the side for Edward. She wrote the book, 'Eighteen Years on Sandringham Estate', which pulled no punches and which is now quite rare, it being rumoured that most copies had been destroyed by the Royal Family.

On Edward's death in 1910, Sandringham House was left to Queen Alexandra and it was to be another 16 years before King George V and Queen Mary were able to take up residence. When George referred to Sandringham as, *"the place I love better than anywhere else in the world,"* he was still occupying York Cottage. When eventually he did move in he made few changes but notably made the first radio broadcast

Appleton House, Norfolk.

to the Empire from here on Christmas Day 1932. He was also to die here in 1936. His eldest son Edward VIII did not have the same attachment to the estate as had his father and younger brother and, in his short lived reign, he only spent one whole day at Sandringham. He effected economies that led to the resignation of his agent Edmund Beck, whose father had also been the agent and lost his life at Gallipoli in 1915. The numbers employed were also reduced. As Edward was life tenant of both Sandringham and Balmoral, George VI was obligated to make a financial settlement which is reported to have approached a seven figure sum.

George VI loved Sandringham as much as his father and reintroduced the family Christmases and continued the Christmas broadcasts. He greatly enjoyed the shooting as has Prince Philip who made his first appearance at Sandringham for the 1946 family Christmas party. George died here on 6th February 1952. The Queen has continued the Christmas tradition and made her first televised broadcast in 1957 from the library. The estate now extends to over 20,000 acres covering the parishes of Anmer, Appleton, Babingley, Birchams, Dersingham, Flitcham, Fring, Sandringham, Shernborne, West Newton and Wolferton. Sandringham had over 365 rooms, reputably more than any other English private house, until, in 1975, 91 of these were demolished to make the house more manageable. Whilst this and other work was carried out, Wood Farm was utilised for the Royal Party. In 1973 the Queen established the museum and in 1977 opened the house to the public. The water tower has been converted into a holiday home run by the Landmark Trust, and Park

House, the birthplace of the late Diana Princess of Wales, is leased to the Leonard Cheshire Foundation as a holiday home for the disabled. Also part of the estate, Anmer Hall was until relatively recently let to the Duke of Kent. Appleton House was the country home of Queen Maud of Norway, George V's sister, until her death in 1938 and was converted to an air raid shelter for use during the second world war.

SENNOWE PARK

Sennowe Hall, Guist.

The estate was acquired in 1898 by Thomas Albert Cook who was the grandson of the founder of the famous travel agents. Cook, who had sold out from the family firm to purchase a sporting estate, clearly required something more fitting than the existing house and commissioned George Skipper to design what is most certainly the most ebullient flamboyant country house to be constructed in East Anglia after the turn of the century. Skipper built the new house around the core of the 5 bay by 5 bay two storey plus attic Georgian existing house which dated from the 1770s.

Skipper, who was born nearby at Dereham, established a practise in Norwich after which he rarely ever needed to work out of the County. Several office buildings in the City show his style, the most well known being that for the Norwich Union Life Office in Surrey Street. He also designed the Royal Arcade, with its Art Nouveau tiling, and several hotels

THE HALL, SENNOWE PARK.

in Cromer, the most well known being the rebuilding of the Hotel de Paris. Skipper was at the height of his confidence as an architect when commissioned by Cook who wanted an expression of his wealth and, after approving the designs, left for a two year world cruise.

For Skipper the commission was prodigious for as well as additions to the hall, there was a complete range of stabling and coach houses, a motor garage, laundry, water tower and electric power house. The entrance

SENNOWE LODGES, GUIST.

forecourt was to be entirely remodelled, the gardens redesigned and enlarged, a nine acre lake with boathouse constructed, new approaches made to the hall with bridges and two new sets of lodges. The result was a baroque extravaganza, some three to four times the size of the original, but which totally succeeded – with just one criticism. 'But where is my ball room?' This omission was soon remedied with the winter garden being enlarged sufficiently to accommodate dancing.

The present owner, Thomas R.E. Cook, a former High Sheriff, is the grandson of the builder and is a champion of rural Norfolk. He took over the estate in 1970 following the death of his father, Sir Thomas who was the MP for North Norfolk from 1931 to 1945.

SHADWELL COURT

Described by Mark Girouard in his 1964 Country Life article as 'a Victorian Cathedral in Miniature', this sensational country house started life as a modest plain Georgian house of the late 1720s, by amateur architect John Buxton who was also responsible for the long demolished Bixley, and Earsham. The Shadwell and Rushford estates, close to Thetford, had been purchased by the Buxton family just after 1600. Robert Buxton, a predecessor, had been in the service of, and received patronage from, the 4th Duke of Norfolk at Kenninghall and had held a lease on the estates. The Buxtons owned the large Elizabethan Channonz Hall at Tibenham and in about 1727 John Buxton commenced work at Shadwell on what was intended as a secondary residence, built perhaps to escape the winter cold at rambling Channonz or as a base to oversee their estate. In any case, soon after John's death in 1731, Shadwell became the family home and Channonz was let, and later considerably reduced, but still owned by the family until sold in the 1930s.

Shadwell was a modest house and the architects Matthew Brettingham, William Wilkins and Sir John Soane were all consulted at various times in the latter part of the 18th century with a view to enlargement. Apart from improvements to the park, nothing was carried out until Sir John Jacob Buxton Bt (the baronetcy had been created in 1800) commissioned Edward Blore to considerably enlarge and reface John Buxton's house in a "jacobethan" style. Sir John did not live to see the work completed and was succeeded by Sir Robert Jacob Buxton who was still a minor.

SHADWELL COURT

In the early 1850s Sir Robert employed the Victorian gothic architect, Samuel Sanders Teulon, to rebuild the parish church at Brettenham, restore the remains of the old college at Rushford as a rectory and build a bridge over a nearby ford. When this was complete Teulon started adding to the house, with liberal use of carrstone, flint and brick to produce what we see today. Sir Robert's mother, the dowager Lady Buxton, when writing to a cousin in America said, *"you will I think be astonished when you see poor dear Shadwell again"*. Sir Robert died in 1888 without a male heir and several years later the house and estate were put up for sale by private treaty. The substantial illustrated catalogue detailed the 11,444 acre estate which included a 200 acre park, extensive lake, Snarehill House, Rushford College, lodges, innumerable farms and cottages all in the parishes of Thetford, Snarehill, Rushford, Brettenham, Bridgham, Roudham and Wretham.

By 1898 John Musker, who was a founder of the Home and Colonial Stores chain, had purchased and created at Shadwell what was to became the largest stud-farm in Europe. He was succeeded by his son Harold and, in turn in 1946, by his son John who was knighted in 1952. He became the chairman at the age of 28 of the banking firm of Cater, Brightwen & Co and was treasurer to the London County Council. He continued the tradition for racing and shooting but by 1984 had sold, for a reported ten million pounds, to the Sheikh Hamdam bin Rashid al-Maktoum, the brother of the ruler of Dubai. The Sheikh, primarily being interested in the stud, allowed the Muskers to continue to live in the house. Sir John died in May 1992 with Lady Musker predeceasing him. The auctioneers, Sothebys, held a two day contents auction at the house in October of that year, and in the following year Sir John's desk, 'the Anglesey Desk', fetched 1.761 million pounds at Christies. The house has since been mainly vacant and is now considered at risk.

SHERINGHAM PARK

Visited by thousands of people each year, who come to marvel at the rhododendrons, wander through the woods and parkland and take a peep at the house, Sheringham Park is a fitting memorial to one of the nation's greatest landscape gardeners – Humphrey Repton.

The Park, and in fact the town and the village, will always be associated with the name of Upcher. In 1809 Abbot Upcher, the surviving son of Peter and Elizabeth Upcher of Ormesby, married Charlotte, the daughter of the Reverend Henry Wilson from Kirby Cane. They soon had a growing family and already with a son, Henry Ramey, and a daughter, Charlotte Mary (they were to have two more of each), this young couple,

IVY LODGE, SHERINGHAM PARK.

both deeply religious and sharing a love for literature, had by 1811 settled upon the estate of Cook Flower at Sheringham for their new home. The price of £52,000 was agreed and on July 10th the agreement was signed with Cook Flower's attorney at Aylsham, a William Repton who was Humphrey's son. In his journal, Abbot Upcher wrote, *"Dined at Mr Repton's; met Mr Repton, his father, the famous planner of grounds &c"*. Almost certainly it was at that dinner where the seeds for Repton's favourite commission were sown.

It was over a year before they were able to take possession, and when they did they stayed at Flower's old farmhouse close to Upper Sheringham which was barely adequate for their increasing family. By July 2nd 1813, two years after the agreement to purchase had been signed, the first stones of the new house were laid. 1817 saw the house nearing completion and the family hoped to move in by the summer, but early in that year, Abbot was struck down with an illness, of which he had intermittingly suffered for many years, and left Sheringham with his family for Kent where he died on 2nd February 1819 at the age of only 35. The Hall remained unfinished and was not complete until 1839 when Henry Ramey moved in at the time of his marriage. Charlotte remained at Cook Flower's old farmhouse and devoted herself to the village, the Church and her family. She died in 1857.

Humphrey Repton, when he presented his proposals in 1812 in the form of one of his famous 'Red Books' illustrated with water colours and text in freehand, stated, *"that I leave this record of such a specimen of my Art, as I never before had an opportunity of displaying : and should these hints be honor'd by your approbation and adoption, this may be considered as my most favorite work . . ."* It was of course a rare commission where he was able, with the assistance of his son John Adey, to design both the house and the landscape.

Henry Morris Upcher inherited in 1892, was succeeded by Henry Edward Sparke Upcher who was knighted, and then by Thomas Upcher in 1954. It was Thomas who erected the Temple which had remained unbuilt from Repton's original scheme. Thomas died a bachelor and in 1986 the estate was purchased by the National Trust who have opened it to the public. Sheringham Hall has been sold on a long lease as a family home and is not generally open.

SHOTESHAM PARK

The Fellowes came to Norfolk in the early 1720s when William Fellowes, a barrister and a Master of Chancery, purchased the 871 acre estate with its rambling moated manor house. With inherited wealth, he was well able to provide for his four sons, one of whom, another William, inherited Shotesham at the age of 19. William's interests, apart from that of the law and acting as member of parliament for Ludlow, were in his estate and in acts of philanthropy, in particular medicine. He founded at Shotesham what was to be England's first 'cottage hospital', where his neighbour, Benjamin Gooch, the surgeon, was able to operate. He also, as 'founder', laid the foundation stone of the Norfolk and Norwich Hospital in 1771.

William died in 1775 and was succeeded at Shotesham by his son Robert, and it was he who engaged (Sir) John Soane in 1784 to draw up plans for a new house some distance from the existing one. Robert, perhaps, was not an easy client for Soane as he expected to be consulted, and had views on, every detail however small. Letton was Soane's first completed country house commission in 1783, but Shotesham remains largely unaltered as one of his best preserved and complete estates. Apart from the house, Soane also designed the offices, stables, walled garden, ice house and a lodge. It is said that one of Robert's first acts, after moving his family into the new house in 1791, was to compile a catalogue

SHOTESHAM HALL, NORWICH.

of his library which had been built up by successive generations. The library was intact when sold for £84,447 when dispersed at auction in 1979, lot one being that same catalogue dated August 1791.

Robert Fellowes died in 1829 and was succeeded by his son, another Robert (1817-1915), who by 1872 had seen the estate grow to 7,758 acres. However, by July 1979, with no male heir and in poor health, Major Charles Fellowes put the house and estate (by now only 1,071 acres) up for auction. It sold for 1.6 million pounds to Danish partners, with the contents, apart from the books, fetching a further £89,000. The house now with 700 acres was again sold in 1989.

STANFIELD HALL

A large ivy clad moated neo-Elizabethan house situated three miles east of Wymondham. A hall at Stanfield was mentioned in the Doomsday Book and there have been several mentions since. It seems possible that parts of an earlier house are still preserved within the existing which was constructed from the 1790s into the 19th century for the Reverend George Preston, initially by the Norwich architect, William Wilkins. The house is chronicled by the late owner, Dr Harold Hudson, in his book entitled 'Stanfield Hall'. Dr Hudson purchased the house in 1947 with 420 acres,

STANFIELD HALL, WYMONDHAM.

increasing this to over 1,000 acres and built up a noted 170 strong beef herd. On his retirement in 1983 he sold to the Stearns who, in turn, put the hall with 34 acres on the market in 2004 but retained the estate.

Stanfield Hall was the scene of one of the most infamous murders of the mid 19th century when James Blomfield Rush shot the owner Isaac Jermy and his son, Isaac Jermy Jermy. Isaac Jermy, who was the Recorder of Norwich, had been George Preston's son and heir (he had changed his name to Jermy by deed poll to satisfy the terms of a will connected with the inheritance of the estate). Rush was arrested the next day and stood trial in Norwich, found guilty and hanged publicly in front of the castle gates. The trial had created enormous interest, special trains were run from London and a huge crowd gathered to see the execution. The trial was extensively reported in the local and national newspapers, books were written narrating the events and the trial, and Staffordshire pottery figures were sold representing the Hall, Potash Cottage (where Rush had lived), Rush and his mistress, Emily Sandford. Such was the rush to market these figures that a representation of Norwich Castle was made with round towers!

STIFFKEY OLD HALL

Associated with the Bacons, Greshams and Townshends and situated in an idyllic setting next to the church and with south facing views over the river valley, this house, conceived in the 16th century and never quite finished nor ever at the hub of a great estate like so many of its contemporaries, nevertheless has survived to take on a sustainable roll suited to the 21st century.

Sir Nicholas Bacon rose to power in the time of Queen Elizabeth who knighted him, made him a privy councillor and Lord Keeper of the Great Seal. In the early 1570s he purchased land at Stiffkey for his second son Nathaniel who lived nearby at Cockthorpe and had married Anne the daughter of Thomas Gresham. Sir Nicholas had given instructions for the building of a four sided house enclosing a courtyard with four towers at the external corners and four more internally and with a series of gardens mathematically planned in relation to the proportions of the house. Building was started in 1576 but was not complete when Sir Nicholas died in 1579. In his will he left only the sum of £200 to, *"Nathaniel, my sonne towards the building of his house at Stiffkey,"* and it was possibly for this reason that the house was not completed as originally intended.

Nathaniel was knighted in 1604, which was the date that the building work was probably completed, and died in 1619, leaving Stiffkey to Roger his grandson. Nathaniel's daughter, Anne, had married Sir John Townshend of Raynham who had been killed in a duel in 1603 and she

Old Hall and Church, Stiffkey.

had brought Roger up at Stiffkey. However, he put his energies into the building of the great house at Raynham and this became the family seat, which it still is. Thus commenced the long decline of Stiffkey, part demolished and probably used as a farmhouse but still owned by the Townshends until they sold in 1911.

The house was resold several times during the 20th century until, in 1978, the then owner, a Miss Esme Greenyer, left the virtually derelict house in eight overgrown acres to a member of the Feilden family who six years before had come across it by chance. Sir Bernard Feilden, the celebrated architect, with his brothers and other family members then restored Stiffkey as a home for four families, living there until 2000 when they placed it on the market for 1.3 million pounds.

STRATTON STRAWLESS HALL

Some houses are of interest not so much for their architecture, but for the people who made their home there. With Stratton Strawless it is the Marshams, or to be exact Robert Marsham the naturalist, who have lived in the area since at least 1100 and originate from the village of the same name. An earlier Robert, in the 14th century, was the first Marsham to live at Stratton Strawless and four centuries later in 1708 another Robert was born, the eldest of eleven, to Thomas Marsham who had married Dorothy Gooch of Earsham Hall.

From an early age Robert developed an interest in natural history and in particular trees. When he was ten he was planting acorns and by fourteen making notes about the birds that he had observed. He attended Clare College Cambridge and on leaving, rather than going out in the world to seek his fortune, he returned to the family home and followed the lifestyle of a young county squire. He became friends with William, son of Ashe Windham at Felbrigg, and also William's tutor Benjamin Stillingfleet with whom he had a shared interest in the study of botany and natural history. They both kept records of the weather and temperature, the migration of birds, the foliation of trees, the progress of crops and other such seasonal vagaries. From 1736, Robert started compiling annual tables of 'the indications of spring' comprising twenty-six of the most familiar occurrences of each spring – the date of the earliest snowdrop and swallow, when a variety of tree came into leaf, the date that rooks built their nests and that frogs croaked and so on. He kept these tables until the year of his death.

The land at Stratton was generally poor, but this seemed to spur Robert to increase his plantations with conifers, oak, chestnut, hornbeam and in particular beech. 1749 saw the birth of Robert, his son and heir, and when in 1751 his father died, he was encouraged by his wife Mary to think about building a new house. A site was selected and possibly thoughts given to style but, in the end, his plantations won over bricks and mortar. In 1790, at the age of 82, Robert discovered a recently published book entitled 'The Natural History and Antiquities of Selborne' which gave him such pleasure that he wrote a long letter to the author, Gilbert White. This lead to a vigorous correspondence between the two elderly naturalists, only ceasing on White's death three years later. Robert Marsham continued to plant, record and experiment with his trees right up to his death at the age of 89 and his Indications of Spring remains as a testament to his long life.

Soon after he inherited, his son built the new house of three storeys with projecting wings. A successor, Charles Marsham, left the estate in 1885 to a cousin, Colonel Edward George Keppel, who sold in 1900 to William John Birkbeck. Much of the timber was felled during the first World War and the estate sold again in 1918. It served as the headquarters for RAF Coltishall during the second World War with an ops room built adjacent and nissen huts in the grounds for RAF and WAAF personnel. This use remained until 1948 which inevitably led to the gardens, shrubberies and parkland becoming uncared for and desolate. The estate, then 506 acres, was offered for auction in November 1949. Lot One comprised the house (including the ops room), stables, entrance lodges, pleasure grounds (with 125 oak, 54 beech, 34 fir and 15 others), all in sixty-three acres. The magnificent Cedar in Reedhouse Grove, of over 200 years of age and reputed the finest and largest in the British Isles, was included in this lot but with a covenant not to be felled.

The house has since been converted into flats with a caravan park surrounding and was reduced in height to two storeys with a flat roof in about 1960. The 1990s have seen the construction of a pitched roof but not the reinstatement of the top floor.

WEST ACRE HIGH HOUSE

The seat of the Birkbecks since 1897 when the estate was purchased from the Hamonds. It has been suggested that, as a nephew, had Henry Birkbeck (1853-1930) not bought the estate then he may well have inherited, though the actual circumstances at the time are not totally clear or perhaps straightforward.

The High House at West Acre was built by 1756 for Edward Spelman who was a bachelor and an eccentric. A contemporary report from a visitor, a Caroline Girle, in 1756 stated, *"I paid a droll visit to see an odd house, of a still odder Mr Spelman, a most strange bachelor of vaste fortune but indeed I'll not fall in love with him. We were introduced to him in the library where he seemed deep in study (for they say he's really clever) sitting in a Jockey Cap in stiff white Dog's Gloves. On seeing Mr Spelman one no longer wonders at the oddity of the edifice he has just finished"*. High House was acquired from Spelman by Richard Hamond in 1761 but he was allowed to stay on as a tenant until he died six years later.

Richard Hamond's nephew, Anthony (1742-1822) from Swaffham succeeded in 1776 and it seems that he added wings with double flight sedan steps to the piano nobile level, as shown in the 1820 engraving for Neales Seats. The country house architect, W.J. Donthorne provided plans for further altering the house for Anthony's son, Philip (1782-1824), who died before they could be put into effect. His successor was Anthony (1805-1869), his second son, who had the house refaced in Holkham brick and demolished the external stairs, presumably replacing them with the present internal double flight. It was Anthony's daughter who married Henry Birkbeck's father in 1849.

The late Captain Harry Birkbeck (1915-2003) in his privately published book 'The Birkbecks of Norfolk' tells the story of the family, how they came to live in Norfolk and at West Acre, their extensive connection with Barclays Bank and the Gurneys, and of the Hamonds and their predecessors. At the time of Captain Birkbeck's death, the estate comprised some 9,000 acres of which one third was in hand with the remaining tenanted. He has been succeeded by his son, Henry Charles.

WOLTERTON HALL

Horatio Walpole was two years younger than his statesman brother Robert, and neither politically nor architecturally did he attain the heights that his brother had reached. Almost certainly aided by Robert, who was effectively Britain's first Prime-Minister, he became an able politician and diplomat both at the Hague and, between 1723 and 1730, as Ambassador in Paris. In 1722 he acquired the estate at Wolterton with its existing old mansion house, which he commenced to renovate. However, in November 1724, a fire destroyed the house in its entirety and, within weeks, Thomas Ripley was called in to advise on rebuilding. In a letter to Walpole, Ripley wrote, *"I think You should put an Entire Stop to all Your Works at Woolterton; Because I believe You will find a More Convenient Place to set Your House in then were it now is, and to answer Your present Gardens, – if You intend to make Woolterton your seat, to order Earth to be thrown up for as many bricks, as possibly can be made next Season; and to buy any oak that is going down near You; that is fitt for Building;"* Ripley had been responsible for the building work at Robert Walpole's great house at Houghton, but was considered unimaginative as an architect*. However, he designed a fine house at Wolterton of pale red brick with the lower floor faced in Portland stone and beautifully situated looking out over the grounds, parkland and the lake designed by Charles Bridgeman. Preparatory works were commenced in the spring of 1725,

but it was not until 1741 that the house was finally completed. In 1756 Horatio was created the 1st Baron Walpole of Wolterton and he died the following year, being succeeded by his son, also named Horatio.

Horatio Walpole, the 2nd baron, was created the 1st Earl of Orford of the second creation in 1806. The original title had died out in 1797 on the death of Robert Walpole's youngest son, Horace who was the 4th and last earl. The 3rd earl of the second creation was another Horatio, and it was he who commissioned George Stanley Repton, the fourth son of the famous landscape gardener Humphrey Repton, to build a new wing to the east and add the stone steps and balustrading with an arcade beneath to the south. After his death in 1858, the 4th earl, again a Horatio, left Wolterton to live at Mannington and the house remained empty until the time of Robert the 5th and last earl who was Horatio's brother's son. He restored the house and moved back from Mannington in about 1905 and died in 1931. He did not have a male heir so the earldom became extinct and the barony and the estate passed to another Robert, a descendant of Thomas Walpole, the brother of Horatio the 1st earl.

Robert, the 7th Baron Walpole, opened the house to the public in 1950, but in 1952 a fire broke out in a second floor bedroom which gutted this floor and seriously water-damaged the rooms beneath. The contents of the state rooms were saved almost in their entirety by the prompt attention of the fire brigade, estate staff and neighbours who, it is said, showed great courage in rescuing the less accessible paintings and furnishings. Lord and Lady Walpole set about restoring the damage and within three years the house was again open to the public. The present owner, the 8th baron (and also 10th Baron Walpole of Walpole), inherited in 1989 and is committed to conservation. Twenty-six estate houses and cottages were put up for auction in May 1989, and in 1997 publicity was given to a possible takeover of both the Wolterton and Mannington estates by the National Trust. However, both estates still remain with the family and access is given to the public.

Horatio Walpole possibly had initial doubts concerning Ripley's ability as an architect as he also took advice from the amateur architect, 11th Earl of Mar, who produced a design for a new house at Wolterton dated April 1725. (PRO Edinburgh, Scottish Record Office).

BIBLIOGRAPHY

The following works are of particular relevance to the study of the Norfolk Country House:

M J Armstrong *History and Antiquities of the County of Norfolk 11 volumes* (1781)
Cromwell *Excursions in the County of Norfolk 2 volumes* (1818/19)
J Grigor *The Eastern Arboretum* (1841)
R H Mason *Norfolk Photographically Illustrated* (1865)
Return of Owners of Land – Norfolk (1871)
E Preston-Willins *Some of the Old Halls and Manor Houses in the County of Norfolk* (1890)
H M Colvin *A Biographical Dictionary of English Architects 1660 – 1840* (1954)
B Cozens-Hardy *Some Norfolk Halls. Norfolk Archaeology Volume 32* (1961)
Burke's & Savills *Guide to Country Houses Volume III. East Anglia* (1981)
G Winkley *The Country Houses of Norfolk* (1986)
P Barnes *Norfolk Landowners since 1880* (1993)
R Wilson and A Mackley *Creating Paradise. The Building of the English Country House 1660 – 1880* (2000)
Whites and Kellys Directories
Burkes and Debretts Peerages
Country Life

Of these Winkley, Burke's & Savills, Cozens-Hardy, Colvin and Burkes Peerage have been in continual use. I have found 'Creating Paradise' to be particularly invaluable for the specific houses that it covers. Also, for 25 years, I have avidly kept articles from the Eastern Daily Press on this subject. These have also been invaluable for the more recent history. I felt sure that they would 'come in handy' one day.

The following source references are those of which I have made the most use. Inclusion is not meant to imply that they are the only or the major works that relate to each house. The date refers to that of the volume used rather than that of the first publication. In all cases the works mentioned are from my own library.

BARNINGHAM
Anon *Leaflet, 2 sides – printed for when the house was open to the public* (Nd)

BAYFIELD
EDP *What's on Magazine* (May 6th 1995)
Larks Press *Sir Alfred Jodrell – Pocket Biographies No 12* (1996)
R Fiske (note by) *Heraldry in Norfolk Churches volume 4* (2004)

BEESTON
Anon *Beeston Hall – Brochure* (Nd)
F Hornor /Knight Frank & Rutley *Estate Sale catalogue* (1994)

BLICKLING

Manuscript/Typescript *Blickling Estate (The Marquis of Lothian) Particulars of rents and outgoings, Inventory, Inland Revenue Valuation Schedule* (1914 – 1930)
R W Ketton-Cremer *Norfolk Portraits – Oliver Le Neve & his duel with Sir Henry Hobart* (1944)
J M Butler *Lord Lothian (Philip Kerr)1882 – 1940* (1960)
National Trust *Blickling Hall* (1987)

CROMER

Baker & Son *Cromer Hall Estate, building plots sale catalogue* (1891)
C Buxton *Memoirs of Sir Thomas Fowell Buxton Bart* (1849)
The Marquess of Zetland *Lord Cromer* (1932)
Hon H A Wyndham *A Family History of the Wyndhams, 2 volumes* (1939/1950)
J Earwaker & K Becker *Literary Norfolk* (1998)
R Owen *Lord Cromer* (2004)

DITCHINGHAM

Anon *Ditchingham Hall* (1988)
Country Life (3/3/1994)

EAST BARSHAM

Irelands *Estate Sale catalogue* (1935)
Phillips *Contents Sale catalogue* (1977)
Strutt & Parker *House Sale catalogue*

FELBRIGG

R W Ketton-Cremer *Felbrigg The Story of a House* (1962)
National Trust *Felbrigg Hall* (1995)

GILLINGHAM

A Hassell Smith, G Baker & R W Kenny *The Papers of Nathaniel Bacon of Stiffkey, volume I, 1556 – 1577* (1979)
D Lindsay *Sir Edmund Bacon A Norfolk Life* (1988)
Brown & Co *Estate Sale catalogues* (1999 & 2000)
Savills *House Sale catalogue* (2005)

GUNTON

R M Bacon *A Memoir of the Life of Edward, Third Baron Suffield* (1838)
A Lowth *My Memories 1830 – 1913 Lord Suffield* (1913)
Irelands *Estate Sale catalogue – outlying portions* (1919)
J M Robinson *The Wyatts an Architectural Dynasty* (1979)
Irelands *Sale catalogues – contents/lodges/Estate properties* (1980 – 82)
M Binney & K Martin *The Country House: To Be or Not To Be* (1982)
Anon *Gunton Tower Past and Present* (Nd)

HANWORTH
Country Life (15/1/1987)

HEYDON
J Preston *That Odd Rich Old Woman, Elizabeth Barbara Bulwer-Lytton of Knebworth House 1773 – 1843* (1998)
H Montgomery-Massingberd & C Sykes *English Manor Houses* (2001)
J Preston *The Squires of Heydon Hall* (2003)

HILBOROUGH
Various Auctioneers *Contents, Estate, Village & House Sale catalogues* (1985 to date)

HOLKHAM
H Montgomery-Massingberd & C Sykes *Great Houses of England and Wales* (1994)
Holkham Newsletters No 1 – 11 (2000/06)
L Schmidt C Keller & P Feversham *Holkham* (2005)

HONING
R W Ketton-Cremer *Norfolk Gallery – Humphrey Repton in Norfolk* (1948)
P Dean *Sir John Soane and the Country Estate* (1999)
R Wilson and A Mackley *Creating Paradise* (2000)

HOUGHTON
R W Ketton-Cremer *Norfolk Gallery – George Walpole – 3rd Earl of Orford* (1948)
S Jackson *The Sassoons Portrait of a Dynasty* (1989)
H Montgomery-Massingberd & C Sykes *Great Houses of England and Wales* (1994)
Anon *Houghton Hall Norfolk* (1996)

HUNSTANTON
D A Jasen *P.G.Wodehouse A Portrait of a Master* (1975)
S C Jenkins *The Lynn and Hunstanton Railway* (1987)
K Fryer *A Fine Strong Boy The Life and Times of Henry L'Strange Styleman Le Strange (1815 – 1862).* (2000)

KEN HILL
Christies/Savills *Contents/House Sale catalogues* (1999)
S Soros & C Arbuthnott *Thomas Jeckyll Architect and Designer 1827 – 1881* (2003)

KETTERINGHAM
O Chadwick *Victorian Miniature* (1960)
E Tisdall *Mrs Pimpernel Atkyns* (1965)
Anon *Tacolneston A Portrait of a Norfolk Village* (2002)
S Soros & C Arbuthnott *Thomas Jeckyll Architect and Designer 1827 – 1881* (2003)

KIMBERLEY
John Earl of Kimberley *The Wodehouses of Kimberley* (1887)
Jackson – Stops & Staff *Estate Sale catalogue* (1958)
J Harris *William Talman Maverick Architect* (1982)
Z Dovey *An Elizabethan Progress* (1996)
R Turner *Capability Brown and the Eighteenth – Century English Landscape* (1999)
R Wilson & A Mackley *Creating Paradise* (2000)
Earl of Kimberley & C Roberts *The Whim of the Wheel The Memoirs of the Earl of Kimberley* (2001)

LANGLEY
Langley School *prospectus* (Various)
Sir C Beauchamp *Copy Letters/npc/telegrams re Sale* (1957)
J D Wood *Estate Sale catalogue* (1957)
D Stroud *Sir John Soane Architect* (1984)
P Dean *Sir John Soane and the Country Estate* (1999)

LETTON
Knight Frank & Rutley *Estate Sale catalogue* (1913)
Irelands *House Sale catalogue* (1979)
G Darley *John Soane An Accidental Romantic* (1999)

LEXHAM
G Cubitt *Contents Sale catalogue* (1911)
Litcham Historical & Amenity Society *The Book of Litcham with Lexham & Mileham* (2002)

LYNFORD
Country Life (28/11/1903)
Humberts *House sale catalogue* (1995)
Savills *House Sale catalogue* (2001)
J Roberts *Glass The Strange History of the Lyne Stephens Fortune* (2003)
G Moore & A Twist *Weeting Worthies* (2004)

MANNINGTON
C Tomes *Mannington Hall and its Owners* (1916)
Anon *Mannington Hall & Gardens* (Nd)
Anon *The Mannington & Wolterton Estate* (1992)

MELTON CONSTABLE
Baron Hastings *Astley of Melton Constable 1236 – 1936* (1936)
J Welcome *Fred Archer His Life & Times* (1967)
D Stroud *Capability Brown* (1975)
Irelands Hall & Palmer *Estate Sale catalogue* (1983)
Strutt & Parker *Estate Sale catalogue* (1986)
R Ketton-Cremer/D Yaxley *Three generations* (1992)
R Turner *Capability Brown and the Eighteenth – Century English Landscape* (1999)

MERTON
Rev G Crabbe *Norfolk Archaeology Volume VI* (1864)
J Ruffer *The Big Shots Edwardian Shooting Parties* (1978)
Anon *Stanford Battle Area* (1979)
B Martin *The Great Shoots Britain's Premier Sporting Estates* (1999)

MIDDLETON TOWER
F Steer *Middleton Tower Norfolk* (1961)

NARFORD
A Moore *Norfolk & The Grand Tour* (1985)

OXBURGH
H Bedingfield *Oxburgh Hall The First 500 Years* (1991)
M Bence-Jones *The Catholic Families* (1992)
Z Dovey *An Elizabethan Progress* (1996)

PICKENHAM
Osborn & Mercer *Estate Sale catalogue* (1924)
J Franklin *The Gentleman's Country House and its Plan 1835 – 1914* (1981)
Knight Frank & Rutley/Christies *Estate/Contents Sale catalogues* (1986)
Knight Frank & Rutley *Estate Sale catalogue* (1993)

QUIDENHAM
V Stuart *The Beloved Little Admiral, Admiral of the Fleet The Hon Sir Henry Keppel GCB OM* (1967)

RACKHEATH
Knight & Sons *Estate Sale catalogue* (1950)
Aldridge Lansdell *House Sale catalogue* (C.1990)
A Healy *The 467th Bombardment Group September 1943 – June 1945* (1993)
Estate Gazette *Law Reports* (1993)
Tops *House Sale catalogue* (1997)
EDP Magazine (19/9/1998)

RAINTHORPE
Anon *Rainthorpe Hall Norfolk The Home of Mr & Mrs George Hastings* (Nd)
J Young *The Country House in the 1980s* (1981)
Smith Woolley/KFR *Estate Sale catalogue* (1994)
Sothebys *Contents Sale catalogue* (1994)

RAVENINGHAM HALL
D Lindsay *Sir Edmund Bacon A Norfolk Life* (1988)

RAYNHAM HALL
V Townshend Durham *Short Guide Historical and Descriptive to Raynham Hall* (1951)
A Moore *Norfolk & The Grand Tour* (1985)
J Harris *The Design of the English Country House 1620 – 1920* (1985)
O Hill & J Cornforth *English Country Houses Caroline 1625 – 1685* (1985)

RIDDLESWORTH
D Osborne *A History of the Borough of Thetford Fire Brigade* (1988)
C Lamb *Riddlesworth Hall A Brief History* (1996)
H Harper *Breckland Portraits Recollections of a Norfolk Parson* (1997)

RYSTON
R Gunther *The Architecture of Sir Roger Pratt* (1979)
SALLE
R Fiske (note by) *Heraldry in Norfolk Churches Volume 4* (2004)

SANDRINGHAM
Cruso *Library Sale catalogue* (1834)
W Simpson *Estate Sale catalogue* (1836)
The Lady Farmer (Cresswell) *Eighteen Years on Sandringham Estate* (1887)
P Hepworth *Royal Sandringham* (1978)
Anon *Sandringham* (1982)

SENNOWE
Norwich School of Art *Architect Exuberant George Skipper 1856 – 1948* (1975)
C Aslet *The Last Country Houses* (1982)

SHADWELL
C Barker *Estate Sale catalogue* (1890)
A Baggs *Channons Hall – Norfolk Archaeology Volume XXXIV* (1966)
M Girouard *The Victorian Country House* (1979)
Sothebys *Contents Sale catalogue* (1992)
A Mackley *John Buxton Norfolk Gentleman and Architect – Norfolk Record Society Volume LXIX* (2005)

SHERINGHAM
E Pigott *Memoir of The Honourable Mrs Upcher of Sheringham* (Nd)
R Ketton-Cremer *Norfolk Gallery – Humphrey Repton in Norfolk* (1948)
National Trust *Sheringham Park* (1998)

SHOTESHAM
Irelands/Savills *Estate Sale catalogue* (1979)
Christies *Contents Sale catalogue* (1979)
A Batty Shaw *Norfolk & Norwich Medicine a Retrospect* (1992)
P Dean *Sir John Soane and the Country Estate* (1999)
R Wilson & A Mackley *Creating Paradise* (2000)
Shotesham Festival Association *Shotesham 2000* (2000)

STANFIELD
H Hudson *Stanfield Hall* (Nd)
EDP Magazine (28/11/1998)
Bidwells *House Sale catalogue* (2004)

STIFFKEY
A Hassell Smith, G Baker & R Kenny *The Papers of Nathaniel Bacon of Stiffkey Volume I, 1556 – 1577* (1979)
Strutt & Parker *House Sale catalogue* (2000)

STRATTON STRAWLESS
R Ketton-Cremer *Norfolk Gallery – Robert Marsham* (1948)
Knight Frank & Rutley *Estate Sale catalogue* (1949)

WEST ACRE
H Birkbeck *The Birkbecks of Norfolk* (1993)

WOLTERTON
R Ketton-Cremer *Wolterton Hall* (1955)
N Walpole *The Walpoles of Wolterton* (1986)
Prudential *Estate Houses Sale catalogue* (1989)
Anon *The Mannington & Wolterton Estate* (1992)
A Klausmeier *Wolterton Hall in Norfolk by Thomas Ripley: on the major work of an Outcast of Architectural History* (2001)